FACING THE LION

FACING THE LION

Writers on Life and Craft

EDITED BY KURT BROWN

BEACON PRESS
BOSTON

Beacon Press
25 Beacon Street
Boston, Massachusetts 02108-2892

Beacon Press books
are published under the auspices of
the Unitarian Universalist Association of Congregations.

03 02 01 00 99 98 97 96   8 7 6 5 4 3 2 1

Royalties for this publication accrue to
the benefit of Writers' Conferences and Festivals,
a national organization of conference directors.

Library of Congress Cataloging-in-Publication Data

Facing the lion: writers on life and craft / edited by Kurt Brown.
p.   cm.
ISBN 0-8070-6209-X
1. Authorship.   I. Brown, Kurt.   II. Series.
PN151.F23   1996   95–47633
808′.02—dc20

For somewhere there is an ancient enmity
between our daily life and the great work.

—Rainer Maria Rilke, "Requiem for a Friend"

CONTENTS

PREFACE

The call to write is one thing. The complex and continuing difficulty of maintaining oneself as a writer is another. It ought to be enough to simply *write* a good story, essay, or poem—that in itself is rare, a highly improbable outcome. The pangs of creation are well documented by writers in every period of literary history. But the struggle to write continues on all fronts—economic, personal, professional—well past the stage of initial composition, no matter how arduous, like a battle that is always being fought in a war that will never end.

Writers face the lion every day: the lion of the blank page; the lion of meager financial returns; the lion of competition and nonrecognition; the lions of envy, exhaustion, and indifference; the lion of intractable imagination and endless drafts; the lion of shrinking audiences; the lion of available space and free time; the Titanic lion of the past; the lions of social and familial responsibility; the lion of class oppression and racism; the lions of illiteracy, censorship, technology, and shabby education; the critical lion, the doubting lion, the scornful lion; the lions of inane and self-destructive literary theories; the lions of corrosive boredom and distraction. And on and on. More lions than you can shake a stick at—as if that would do any good. The writer enters the arena, and the lions are let loose.

This is not to idealize writers who, being human, are as fallible, weak, imperfect, and vulnerable as anyone else. Nor is it to claim unique status for the writing field as a place of struggle and difficult accomplishment. It is only to point out those particular problems every writer must face and overcome before sitting down to address the ordinary, yet daunting problems of creating something worthy of being published and read. And often, when you succeed, no one notices or cares (even in the writing community itself): writing is one of the only fields were you can succeed, and succeed truly, yet still fail in the larger arena of popular culture and commercial reward.

More than anything else, this third edition in the *Writers on Life and Craft* series addresses the problem of facing the lion. Many of the lectures here record one aspect or another of that fundamental situation and the relentless struggle that ensues. Some do not, or do so only tangentially. But the idea that merely writing well is the artist's sole responsibility and concern has seen its day. That would only be true of a culture that supported writing as an activity instrinsically valuable in itself. More and more, the writer's attention is turning toward dangers that threaten the very existence of language and books in our world, and in any future world we can readily imagine. The lions are everywhere, and they are not going away.

Kurt Brown
Writers' Conferences and Festivals
September, 1995

PAUL ALLEN

Else and Other: A Nonwriter Addresses the Nonwriters at a Writers' Conference

[CHARLESTON WRITERS' CONFERENCE]

Shall any be his own artificer?
—St. Augustine, *Confessions*

All my life I wanted to be somewhere else. As a kid, I would stand in the backyard of Debbie Moss's house watching the sun go down over a line of pines, a grassy field, and then the dark hardwoods that marked the edge of the Alabama River—if I could just get there, could just get out there while the sun's still red, across the river before I would be missed at dusk, if I could just get far enough past the things I knew, far enough out there, then I would be there. I would be There. This is not something one shares with the playmates who have to go home for dinner and are already up to the road. Often as not, my dog would have given up on me and gone back to sleep by my bike.

But if I could be someplace else, I could be someone else. Shane, Randolph Scott. I could save people who deserved saving, demure women who had earned a lift down from the carriage and bald store owners too pitiful for even my do-good dad to pity.

High school, I played baritone horn (in the wimpy treble clef). Nobody hides better than a band member. You skip PE and you don't dress out, and if you're not any good there are no solos. You breathe the tangy air through the gurgling tubes on the forty-yard line; you listen to Doreen on trumpet, Troy on trombone, and you can almost believe you're making music. The uniform helps. Not having to dress out for PE helps. Purple Jesus helps.

In college I wanted to be Bob Dylan, Tom Paxton, Lightnin' Hopkins, Lawrence Ferlinghetti, Bob Dylan, Carl Sandburg, Cisco Houston, Walt Whitman, Holden Caufield, Byron, and Joan Baez. Did I mention Bob Dylan? I wanted my teeth to rot like I thought Bob Dylan's teeth rotted, the way it made him mumble and spit words. They were all out there, ridin' trains, singin' songs, changin' the world. Bein'. Being someone, somewhere else.

And I managed it sometimes, more often than I care to (or can) remember—as long as I had a flask of Scotch, some speed, Camel filters, hypoglycemia (Screw you, draft board!), and a new set of guitar strings with an E flat harmonica in a neck brace tight enough to stay up throughout "With God on Our Side."

Yet when I cut class to wander downtown trying to look like Dave van Ronk might look against a building, when I leaned against the light post, propped a booted toe against the fire hydrant in front of the capitol, and pictured where the civil rights marchers would be gathered in a few days (without me—school policy), I really was missing English 320 with Al, that four-point, prissy, outrageous, stuttering, lovely classmate who made the Cavalier poets cavalier. (I hear Al died of AIDS in Brooklyn last year.)

Ridin' a freight to Only-God-Knows-Where is no fun when you get splinters in the knees and hands trying to stand up in order to breathe the stars, when you go to Only-Everybody-Knows-Where jerking around for hours in a yard car, you learn, that never leaves the industrial area. And the dawn's coming, and the liquor's wearing off. And you are not in Oklahoma. You have to call a little pissant freshman to come get you so you can go back and write your term paper on *Plessy v. Ferguson.* (I was making a D in Sociology 270, "Race Relations," while Joan Baez and Peter, Paul & Mary were less than a mile down Fairview Avenue at St. Jude's. Protestin'.)

Teaching high school, no difference. All through "Thanatopsis" I wanted to be in Earl's head, the lanky Indian boy who, on a horse in the county rodeo, was no longer rider, the horse no longer horse. The dullard kid and the farting beast became one thing, a glistening, breathing creature, noon, casting no shadow. My God, you should have seen Earl when everything about him damned my five subtle ties, my Cross pen I would not let students use.

Graduate school we ate grits with bugs. Wild dogs got in the house. Connie tried to run away, but a big field rat chased her back home. Bathroom floor was too rotted to support us, so we had to shower on the open back porch with a hose hooked up to the kitchen sink. The refrigerator door closed with a two-by-four. And so hot we put the fan on us, letting it blow over ice cube trays and wet towels. And it was still 90–100 degrees inside. Rain blowing through the cracks in the walls. Bills piled up, checks bounced. Oh to be settled in a job, professing! Leather patches on the elbows of my herringbone. Perhaps a pipe and cold weather and a fireplace.

Bills piled up? We had a puppy that got sick. We took him to the university clinic and were told to give him this medicine and to feed him boiled hamburger meat and rice. I remember the meal where the puppy on our floor got his prescribed meat and rice, and my wife and I ate rice. We didn't have enough money for meat for all of us. Oh to be settled in a job, selling in a blue suit with a car that didn't make us turn off the radio and play "guess the cost of the sound."

All the time hating home and school, wanting to be someone, somewhere else, hating anything I was doing because obviously it was keeping me from doing the something else that I could do well, the something else that would make me happy and keep me contented.

Poetry writing got in the way of being a poet. Study and reading interfered with my being a scholar. The broken faucet interrupted my being the good husband. Students got in the way of my teaching.

I thought I was alone, but I wasn't. There is a nation of us, people who think that only major changes—westward movement, conquering—are of value. Or industrialization or damming rivers to change the lay of the land itself. *Something Else or Bust* is still painted on every car we buy on credit. We are dominated by the sense that success, happiness—whatever we are looking for—must be predicated on major changes in our lives, in those around us, in our world.

How many of us have gone to writers' conferences looking for the one "secret" that made the real writers successful? "When do I get the information," we ask at breakfast during second day's registration, "that will change my life? I'm paying the price—$75.00 plus $30 to have a real writer look at my story, and through the magic of marginalia turn me into someone else, the writer." (We never think to ask how much permanent change we get at Waves and Breezes for a physical makeover for the same price. Do we then go directly to the local casting office and say, "I had a $95 makeover at Waves and Breezes. Where is my script?")

We come by it naturally, I suppose, our culture coming from various readings or misreadings of the Bible: Saul of Tarsus struck blind and becoming Paul; Gideon thinking he was too lowly, then watching his army go through seemingly silly tests to be reduced to a paltry "band." "Sell everything, give the money to the poor, and follow me." Move to New York City, get another degree. Always the great American START OVER.

> ... a nation that is no longer one but only an amorphous collection of failed dreams, where we have been told too often by contractors, corporations and prudes that our lives don't matter
>
> —Hugo, "Letter to Oberg"

So off to the University of Florida to learn the craft from John Frederick Nims. I don't think I ever wrote a poem John Nims truly liked. Twenty years later, he still likes me personally, I hope, though he doesn't think much of me as a poet. Calls me a raconteur. Wants to know why I don't write anecdotes. For years I wanted to be a poet of the Nims, Robert Fitzgerald, Hecht, Ciardi ilk—scholar-poets, smart, well read. I was afraid to keep up with Bob Dylan's latest music, he not being a "real" poet.

In *The Writing Life*, Annie Dillard talks about her overly committed youth. Working intently on an early book, she let all her houseplants die:

> After the book was finished I noticed them; the plants hung completely black dead in their pots in the bay window. For I had not only let them die, I had moved them. During that time, I told all my out-of-town friends they could not visit for a while.
>
> "I understand you're married," a man said to me at a formal lunch in New York my publisher had arranged. "How do you have time to write a book?"
>
> "Sir?"
>
> "Well," he said, "you have to have a garden, for instance. You have to entertain." And I thought he was foolish, this man in his seventies, who had no idea what you must do. But the fanaticism of my twenties shocks me now. As I feared it would.

In a rather silly essay in *Northwest Review*, Richard Kostelanetz discusses being, or not being, in the academy, how his life is the right one for a writer. Enough people take him to task that I don't plan to get into that argument. I would like to quote him, though, because one comment is the kind of self-serving, idiotic statement that we nonwriters run across often and, if we don't know we are not writers, begin to believe. We begin to wonder whether we need to "Pick up Stakes," "Poet or Bust," and otherwise live out some bumper sticker *summum bonum.*

Kostelanetz argues that being unaffiliated, he is the business he runs. That's fine, except: "Thankfully, there is neither a family nor a car to support." I wanted to italicize a word of this quotation so I could put in brackets "italics mine," which always makes me feel muscular. I tried *thankfully* then *neither,* then *family, nor, car, to support.* No one word would do: "Thankfully, there is neither a family nor a car to support"?! I am stopped dead by this sentence. There was a time I might have envied his being able to say that, but I know now that Kostelanetz and I have nothing to talk about. I have a family "to support." My problem was never how to get rid of them for good; it was how do I face the fact that I need them? Any of us nonwriters know we can get drunk, drive off, and start another life. We also know that as soon as we started that other life, we'd want the old one back. Or we'd start wanting still another one. I can learn nothing from such a man.

Like many, Grace (A. G.) Mojtabai seems to take the high road to art in her essay, "To Actualize the Possible: The Writer in the World." She says, "I believe that artists have a special relationship . . . with life. . . . Not a life of total withdrawal, but a life of frequent, if intermittent, retreat from the world." But I think she is still offering an either/or choice that simply defeated me. I know that some people can dip in and out of roles, or choose one exclusively. I also know—I know now—that I am not one of them.

There are many who can fully commit themselves to the art, even if that commitment is, in Mojtabai's words, "a life of frequent, if intermittent, retreat from the world." Or worse, they commit themselves to themselves as artist. Annie Dillard reminds us that "Jack London claimed to write twenty hours a day." And London died a second-rate writer and a first-rate drunk, didn't he? The list is endless of those great artists who thought art would get them "there." Plath, Hemingway, Faulkner, Twain, Sexton, Berryman, Sinclair Lewis, Poe, Capote, Toole . . . One doesn't live such a life, or end it, because the writing does or doesn't come. One drinks like that or agonizes like that, turns that bitter, searching for some new state, some "click that makes everything smooth out" as Brick puts it in *Cat on a Hot Tin Roof*. (Yikes! This is the second time in as many essays that I've quoted that line, and I truly hate the play. Actually I hate all of Tennessee Williams's plays.) Tennessee Williams is another; put him on that list.

For a Christian, the "place" is "the Peace of God which passeth all understanding." For Joseph Campbell it is your "Bliss Station." Whatever it is called by any people or person, it is some metaphysical "Other" which lies outside all our temporal someone else's somewhere else. I am not talking about a humming, guru dream state from which I must return in order to perform a real life in a real world. It is an Other that supersedes that state even.

I've learned that I cannot reach that place through a thorough commitment to art. It would require negating other gifts and blessings, blessings which at one time or another I thought were curses—family, home, country, students. I can't "fly by those nets" for art as Stephen Dedalus can at the end of *A Portrait of the Artist as a Young Man*. While trying to be the writer, I would be eaten up with guilt that my family was being neglected. To be the family man, I would be eaten up with the obsession to write. And on and on. I know; I tried.

What I learned by failing at the total commitment of writer, or husband, or teacher is that I'm not the world's best at any of them, and no one of them of itself even temporarily brings me anything other than anxiety in the face of the others. Unlike the youthful, enthusiastic Dedalus, I must consider art too, a net I must fly by.

Unless a man be born again

Dangerous stuff, that, turning biblical principles of spirit into worldly principles of economics, steps to success, or a vision for a country's destiny.

We nonwriters need to remember that most gold mines for which people pulled up stakes and left everything didn't pan out. Former shop owners finally set up shop again. The dentist who wanted gold ended in Sacramento, buying it, to put in Californians' mouths instead of the mouths of his friends in Virginia Beach. The magic didn't happen. And some, some, pitifully, kept panning in wrong places, no joy, no delight, finding some pretty interesting things and slinging them to the ground, looking for someone else's gold. And they became bitter.

We all know them. There are likely a few among us at every writers' conference, the sad ones still dipping their pans in the same mud hole, bitter and full of excuses, and finding fault with the gold others find. They gather in small groups and curse the lack of rain, blame their children. They skip sessions in order to convince each other that there is some magic, some clue, some key that the mean-spirited writers and editors aren't letting them in on. You can hear them, paired off in the opposite corner from the book-sale table, hissing "It's who you know. It's who you know. It's who you know."

They are more right than they believe. It is who you know:

> The thing about bitches is knowing *you* are.
> —Ciardi, "Bitches"

Knocked down no matter which banner I lifted from a pile of corpses, I now have to check in, often and alone, asking, "What fruit is this action bearing?" Do my writing or teaching or fathering or husbanding actions at any given moment breed discord, jealousy, fits of rage, selfish ambition, dissension, factions, and envy?

They used to. Each of my adopted personae used to bring on restlessness, bitterness. Why? Because it wasn't one of the other personae.

Here's my Donald Hall story. Back in the early '80s, I brought Donald Hall to my campus for a reading and workshop. The good-natured "me" invited Wendy Salinger, who lived nearby, to the different functions, since Hall had recently picked her book for the National Poetry Series winner. (I was nothing if not gracious, particularly when I didn't have a manuscript to send out.) After the reading, cocktails at a person's house. But I got to drinking a lot, and with a couple of others ranted about the incompetence of some of our colleagues . . .

> When serpents bargain for the right to squirm
> —cummings

. . . who in fact scared me (that is, the-new-instructor-wanting-to-be-a-scholar me). Finally Wendy left in a huff, the titular objects of our attack being friends of hers. Hall, quite soon after, graciously said it was time to be going. By then I was angrier still at this poet who was enjoying Wendy's conversation, angry at poetry, angry at this life of putting up posters for poets, at the olives and canapés I served poets, at the colleagues who, I felt, were mean and thus made me mean, at my wife and daughters at home, loving me as they slept. Also by then I was quite drunk. Taking Hall back to his hotel, I ran over a curb, as I remember. For years I had a claim to fame—I was one of those who had a rift with a real poet. Wallace Stevens and Archibald MacLeish! The problem was, of course, I'd managed the rift without the aesthetics, without writing anything bold and "rifty." I just embarrassed myself. (That is, I embarrassed all the "my-selves" except one: the put-upon, misunderstood poet unappreciated by people who liked Wendy Salinger's written and published poems better than they liked my truly powerful, albeit unwritten, work.)

Fellow nonwriters, after more liquor and hate and anger than I could hold, I broke like an old home movie. I had to stop thinking if-I-only-had-time (or better support, other paper, new computer, quiet, privacy, money, snow, blow, Bourbon, darkness, light, a room of my own). My peace lay in having to learn a hard lesson: If you had more time, privacy—whatever—you would be exactly where you are right now.

I began learning that we don't have to be struck blind on the road to Damascus, sell our goods, change our lives completely. The ethic which tells us that we and the world need to be made new seems to overlook other passages.

Despite all the anecdotes about absolute commitment to art, sacrificing everything, reestablishing yourself on the continent, we don't have to beat down the walls of Jericho with our own small fists. If we aren't catching anything, we don't have to pull ashore and, say, begin making tents; we can simply try our net on the other side of the boat. Martha, keep doing what you're doing; Mary, do what you're doing. Just don't doubt its value or worry that you ought to be doing the other's activity.

In an essay dealing with the poet's language and the audience/poet relationship, Michael Blumenthal uses the obvious reading of Frost's "Birches" as metaphor. "Birches" he says, "speaks to us of the desire, at times, to substitute a gentler, more pastoral, reality for the harsher one of everyday life; of the wish . . . [to] live in a world of our own imaginings, far from the realities of ice storms and personal loss. But the poem is . . .

memorable and beautiful above all for its willingness to *return* to the world, and to the reality from which it so longed to escape."

It seems to me that Blumenthal is ignoring another "world," that of the persona who does not walk over there, climb a birch, drop. Unlike his action in "I'm going out to clear the pasture spring," in "Birches" the persona seems content to witness from a distance. He likes to think about doing both—leave earth, come back—but does neither. For me, the poem is even more "memorable and beautiful" because the voice doesn't "do" anything, stays put, enjoys passively.

Perhaps another poem's metaphor makes the analogy for me better. In "A Valediction Forbidding Mourning," Donne's argument goes that if the two lovers being parted are, in fact, not one soul like "gold to airy thinness beat," but two individual souls, then they are two

> As stiffe twin compasses are two,
> Thy soule the fixt foot, makes no show
> To move, but doth, if the'other doe.

I take the standard reading of this image. But it does offer a metaphor I can use to help me think through my point. Whether the legs of the compass are lover/lover, as they are here, or are metaphor, as I'm using them, for artist/husband, husband/father, father/teacher, teacher/Episcopalian, each soul is joined to the other at the vertex, something that is neither of the two. For Donne, the hinge is the metaphysical, that which is, was, and always will be. The vertex of his compass is God, the great I Am. If each lover were to marry himself directly to the other lover, commit him or her self to the personhood of the other lover, there would be no flexibility. The relationship could not "admit impediments." But if each is attached to the vertex, something that is neither of the two, then separation and return are possible.

If I attach my various "me's" to the vertex—the Other—than all my nouns (husband, poet, teacher) become verbs. I teach. I write some poems. I fix a thing or two around the house.

I'm not the great *I Am*, but I am my *I am* (as in Frost's "Iota Subscript"), and I accept that none of these activities is who I am. And if any one of them (or all) had to be consciously and willfully sacrificed in order to preserve my relationship to the vertex, to the Other, so be it. Each brings joy only if I don't ask it to, only if I see it as a minor activity under a larger peace.

Under that larger peace my daughter's basketball game is just my daughter's basketball game, not some display of my fatherhood. Sometimes I think about poems during the games. I forgive myself for being "here." And I forgive myself for not being "there." If the image is in my head when I sit down to write, great—I will write it. If not, I don't worry about it. It will come whenever, if ever. I write a poem; I don't write a poem. Big damn deal. I'm not going to be miserable while doing something because I'm haunted by what I'm not doing.

> From this hour I ordain myself loos'd of limits and imaginary
> lines
> —Whitman, "Song of the Open Road"

But with this ordination comes a caveat: I can't be bothered and feel hurt if the world doesn't like what I'm doing or not doing, doesn't sit at the feet of my "loos'd" self. I can't work on poems or parenting as second to my relationship to that sense of Other and expect the product to be first in the world or to get the same credit as the work of those who in fact are more committed than I. As John Ciardi says in "Survival": "I welcome any recognition so long as I am not required to take it seriously. What I do is done for the doing. I am rich so long as I am able to do what pleases me most, if only to fly paper airplanes into the apocalyptic wastebasket. And let the wastebasket remain the central monument to my life."

In a fine essay wrestling with the activity of writing a poem, Stephen Dunn says, "What I wish to say is that the farther we go in a poem or on the ice the fewer and fewer choices we have. . . . Only if we've been compositionally sloppy do we have manifold choices at the end of the poem. Prufrock cannot suddenly become Don Juan."

So too with our lives as writers—as nonwriters. I've been writing poems since I was eighteen. There is a limit now, thirty years later, to the kind of poet I can be. I cannot become the young writer screwing enamored students after a reading, I cannot become a dramatist, I cannot become a lyric poet, a political poet, a scholar poet, a poet who keeps a calendar and acts as agent for his own budding career. It is not too late, however, to write some poems I like writing, work for that peace, for that Other, because my attempting each role full time through the years (and failing at whichever one I wasn't doing at the time) has been my journey on the ice. My options are limited. The poem and the life. The life is the poem.

I return to Dunn's essay, letting "poem" be the metaphor for living:

[Working with the form of a poem] is some happy combination of the poet's intent and the poem's *esprit* and the necessary compromises between the two. We can't be too willful, but we must have things in mind. We don't want to be the wimps of our own poems, but we'd be happy to be led into some lovely places. And we'd like to have some control after we lose control, at least enough to throw light on what has just happened, perhaps even to articulate what it has meant to us. And of course there are moments when we'd be better off being appreciatively silent.

Maybe all my fancy, capitalized "Other" is only this, this kind of silence.

Thinking begins with silence—the simple awareness of the world and oneself in it.
                                                                    —Oppen

And maybe if some modern Puritans, goal-setting-life-planning-free-enterprisers want to call it being beaten into sloth, lethargy, acquiescence, or laziness, so be it.

That kid's wanting to be somewhere else was actually a burn for the Other all along, a yearning for whatever it is that lay outside all activity, places, selves, prayers, dreams, or Saturday matinees.

[The poet] needs to establish his life; to push his way in and out of a number of paper bags—which however should not be too damn papery—and to encounter choices and to acquire himself. And what he does care about and what he doesn't.
                                                                    —Oppen

There was nothing, no peace, I always thought, except through some me doing something else somewhere else, some one me which obviously I had not found.

But there is. There is simply the peace outside all of them. So now I measure my current activity (my verbs, since I've given up the nouns) by way of the sense of joy, peace, patience, self-control each gives me. If I were to feel angry or bitter or put upon while mowing the grass, I'd leave that mower right in midrow and walk off the job until I felt like finishing. I'm not "a mower," either.

>Intelligence is the ability to experience value.
>
> —Oppen

Writing the poem, sweating a copper tube, watching my wife shoo the cat, listening to my daughter's recounting the excellent play of some friend—these have no degree of value, no hierarchical value. They are things I enjoy while I experience value outside them, while I experience a greater peace which none of them gives me if I think of each solely as a self I ought to be. Door number four, none of the above.

>Where truth and virtue are threatened,
>I must surrender even my favorite jewels.
> —Lu Chi, "The Masterpiece"

As I was writing this, my wife broke into my precious work to ask me to come help her find her duster. I did help, briefly, but told her I was only going to make a quick run-through the usual places and quit. It wasn't because my work was more important. As Ciardi says in "Survival," "I write unimportant poems because I am human and gross and have nothing to say." It was because I felt put upon and angry. Anger is not a luxury I can afford—it is bad fruit that brings days of stink and flies to my home and interferes with my relationship to that larger Other.

I offer one last quotation from Ciardi's "Survival." Here again, I grant myself the indulgence of using a poet's description of writing poetry as a metaphor for living the life of the nonwriter who writes poems when he feels like it:

The language [the life of "peace which passes understanding," the life of "following your bliss"] is wiser, deeper, more sentient, and more haunted than anyone who uses it. I mean only to woo [it], to submit myself to it as best I can, and to hope that when I have hearkened to it humbly and gratefully, it will now and then empower me to do what I could never have done when I was important and came to [it] with a half-prepared speech. . . . It is a stirring awake . . . in a haunted silence. It is not an assertion but a being, a hearkening to being, and a way of being.

As is the minor life of someone who no longer thinks of himself as a writer or a teacher or a husband or a father, no longer tells himself that he could be great at one if the others would just back off. I wouldn't be. Besides, I wouldn't want any of them to "back off." I'm going for a walk now.

JANE HIRSHFIELD

Facing the Lion: The Way of Shadow and Light in Some Twentieth-Century Poems

[NAPA VALLEY WRITERS' CONFERENCE]

Stevie Smith once wrote that every poem could be titled either "Heaven, a Detail" or "Hell, a Detail." What I would like to look at here is the relationship between the two—the way the poetry of heaven and the poetry of hell speak to one another and require one another, and the way that what transpires between the realm sometimes called shadow and the realm sometimes called light ripens us, as human beings and as writers, into a more fully realized being. I'd like to enter these questions by looking first at a small poem by Yeats, "The Choice":

> The intellect of man is forced to choose
> Perfection of the life, or of the work,
> And if it take the second must refuse
> A heavenly mansion, raging in the dark.
> When all that story's finished, what's the news?
> In luck or out the toil has left its mark:
> That old perplexity an empty purse
> Or the day's vanity, the night's remorse.

At first reading, the poem is about the familiar figure of the artist alone in his or her tiny garret, about the day-to-day sacrifices and the long-term forgoing of certain ordinary kinds of happiness that the life of art so often requires of its practitioners. But I think there is another way to read the poem as well, and a second knowledge to be taken from it. If you want to write, this other reading says, if you want to pursue the perfection of the work, you must refuse beauty, refuse paradise and ease, and be willing to enter the life of "raging in the dark." This may be one of those places where it seems that a poem tells us more than its author first intended— the first reading is probably what was meant. Yet the wisdom of the second interpretation seems, to me at least, undeniable. It begins to chart a course for us of what we must do and who we must become if we want to perfect and ripen our work.

Especially in the twentieth century, one of the central projects of art has in fact been to enter the part of human experience that Jung referred to as the shadow—to look at what is most difficult, to press by means of both subject matter and new formal techniques into the places of sorrow, chaos, indeterminacy, anger, and the point where madness and imagination meet. I do not think that there is any more shadow in our lives now than there was in the past, but certainly we are more aware of it *as* shadow. There were many previous paintings of war, for example, yet *Guernica* shows it in a new understanding of sheer fragmentation and terror. One of the great shifts in human consciousness of the twentieth century is that we no longer have a conception of nobility that is not haunted, or of beauty that is not terrifying. We know that every gift comes with its price.

This is knowledge which has come to fuller consciousness, but it is not of course new. Dante's journey to Paradise begins in just the opposite direction: it opens with the loss of way and of self to fear and despair in the middle of his life, and occurs according to the ancient Heraclitean rule that the way up is the way down. *The Divine Comedy* maps it clearly: the poet cannot achieve integration without passing first through each of the circles of hell, without seeing for himself what it means to be in limbo, in icy despair, in terror and pain. Earlier is the Greek myth of Prometheus— because he brought to humankind the gift of fire, he is condemned to lie through eternity chained on the top of a mountain, his liver torn out by an eagle. The story tells us that what lights the darkness bears a terrible cost. All the many variations of the Osiris story, including that of Persephone and Demeter, speak of necessary descent into dismemberment or death before the return to a life which is no longer understood as innocent or guaranteed, but as cyclical, bargained for, and provisionally won back.

And there is also the tale of Eve, whose surrender to the desire for knowledge unleashed upon herself and her descendants the myriad sufferings of birth and death and existence subject to time.

Almost everywhere we look we can find examples of this theme: wisdom, at least in the West, is obtained through transgression and paid for in suffering. The journey into maturity, whether seen in Odysseus or Aeneas or Persephone, must take us through the underworld realms of uncertainty, fear, and death before the green and peaceful life we desire and seek can be restored to us—and both world and self are irrevocably changed by the passage through the realm of shadow. Deception, too, is often a part of the course: craftiness and trickery are involved in the test— we are tricked into falling, and tricked into wisdom. It is worth pausing to note the word, craftiness. The beauty of art—its craft—is the trickery with which we come to terms with silence, ignorance, and the inner and outer faces of death.

The theme is not as clear-cut in Eastern traditions. Still, in one of the Jataka stories (traditional Indian folktales about the past lives of the Buddha, showing the various exemplary stages of his path to awakening) the Buddha, finding himself on a mountain ledge above a starving tigress and her ravenous cubs, throws himself into her jaws in order to save her life. In this case, it is in the service of a different kind of ripening—the development of a limitless, selfless compassion rather than of wisdom per se— that the descent into death is required; but the story seems to me to be part of the same genre.

I have become interested in this image of giving oneself to the lion and to the tiger—and more poems touch on it than you might at first imagine. Here is a first, rather odd example, a poem by Stevie Smith:

THE PHOTOGRAPH

They photographed me young upon a tiger skin
And now I do not care at all for kith and kin,
For oh the tiger nature works within.

Parents of England, not in smug
Fashion fancy set on rug
Of animal fur the darling you would hug,

For lately born is not too young
To scent the savage he sits upon,
And tiger-possessed abandon all things human.

This is surely a version of the story, don't you think? The poem suggests that what makes an artist (which means, at least in part, a person whose life is dedicated to the developing process, just as a photograph is) is being exposed—even for the briefest moment—to the tiger. You may think that you are choosing only a decorative background for a baby picture, the poem warns, but you will end up with a child devoured: after this first contact, nothing will keep the tiger nature suppressed, and the savage pursuit of truth becomes more important than kindness, than connection, than any ties. Parents do not want their children to become artists because they know this. They fear not only for the child's outer well-being (remember "The Choice" telling us that the artist will inevitably end up with an empty purse), but also for the havoc the pursuit will wreak, not only upon the child's inner life but upon themselves. A savage spirit raging in the dark does not sit lightly and easily through Thanksgiving dinners; it refuses to charm, to comply, to go to bed at a reasonable hour, to bend to the ways of the world.

I'd like next to offer a longer poem about the process of giving yourself over to the lion, Allen Ginsberg's "The Lion for Real":

THE LION FOR REAL

Soyez muette pour moi, Idole contemplative . . .

I came home and found a lion in my living room
Rushed out on the fire-escape screaming Lion! Lion!
Two stenographers pulled their brunette hair and banged
   the window shut
I hurried home to Paterson and stayed two days.

Called up my old Reichian analyst
who'd kicked me out of therapy for smoking marijuana
"It's happened," I panted "There's a Lion in my room"
"I'm afraid any discussion would have no value" he hung up.

I went to my old boyfriend we got drunk with his girlfriend
I kissed him and announced I had a lion with a mad gleam in
      my eye
We wound up fighting on the floor I bit his eyebrow and he
      kicked me out
I ended masturbating in his jeep parked in the street
      moaning "Lion."

Found Joey my novelist friend and roared at him "Lion!"
He looked at me interested and read me his spontaneous
      ignu high poetries
I listened for lions all I heard was Elephant Tiglon
      Hippogriff Unicorn Ants
But figured he really understood me when we made it in
      Ignaz Wisdom's bathroom.

But next day he sent me a leaf from his Smokey Mountain
      retreat
"I love you little Bo-Bo with your delicate golden lions
But there being no Self and No Bars therefore the Zoo of
      your dear Father hath no Lion
You said your mother was mad don't expect me to produce
      the Monster for your Bridegroom."

Confused dazed and exalted bethought me of real lion
      starved in his stink in Harlem
Opened the door the room was filled with the bomb blast of
      his anger
He roaring hungrily at the plaster walls but nobody could
      hear him outside thru the window
My eye caught the edge of the red neighbor apartment
      building standing in deafening stillness

We gazed at each other his implacable yellow eye in the red
      halo of fur
Waxed rheumy on my own but he stopped roaring and bared
      a fang greeting.
I turned my back and cooked broccoli for supper on an iron
      gas stove

boilt water and took a hot bath in the old tub under the sink
 board.

He didn't eat me, tho I regretted him starving in my
 presence.
Next week he wasted away a sick rug full of bones wheaten
 hair falling out
enraged and reddening eye as he lay aching huge hairy head
 on his paws
by the egg-crate bookcase filled up with thin volumes of
 Plato, and Buddha.

Sat by his side every night averting my eyes from his hungry
 motheaten face
Stopped eating myself he got weaker and roared at night
 while I had nightmares
Eaten by lion in bookstore on Cosmic Campus, a lion myself
 starved by Professor Kandinsky, dying in a lion's
 flophouse circus,
I woke up morning the lion still added dying on the floor—
 "Terrible Presence!" I cried "Eat me or die!"

It got up that afternoon—walked to the door with its paw on
 the wall to steady its trembling body
Let out a soul rending creak from the bottomless roof of his
 mouth
Thundering from my floor to heaven heavier than a volcano
 at night in Mexico
Pushed the door open and said in a gravelly voice "Not this
 time Baby—but I will be back again."

Lion that eats my mind now for a decade knowing only your
 hunger
Not the bliss of your satisfaction O roar of the Universe how
 am I chosen
In this life I have heard your promise I am ready to die I
 have served
Your starved and ancient Presence O Lord I wait in my room
 at your Mercy.

The whole story resides in this poem. The lion enters, we run away, we try everything to distract ourselves, our friends don't believe what we tell them; then the unavoidable battle of wills, the surrender. And more—to be rejected then, forced into a surrender that must be deepened and deepened before the vow is accepted. For giving yourself to the lion, or to poetry, is a vow—nothing more, nothing less than your entire life will be asked.

This poem also clarifies something: the lion is not simply the id. Sex, hunger, dreams—none of these is "the lion for real," they are what Ginsberg turns to in his various attempts to face or not face the lion. The lion for real is a being much more complex, more multi-dimensional, and more outer. Not simply some untamed part of the self, it is an untamed part of the world, something we can't own or control, something we eventually have to acknowledge because its presence in our lives is irrefutable and overwhelming and transformative—if we will let it be.

A first impulse is to say that giving yourself to the lion is a matter of courage, and to some extent it is. Every time we sit down to write, we open our house to strangers, not knowing whether what enters will be the disguised god of so many myths or the disguised demon of so many fairy tales; both of them, we eventually must learn, come bearing gifts. But still, it is not only courage that is required. Remember that Ginsberg doesn't—can't—get away with a single flamboyant gesture. The path to resolution of the situation is closer to a kind of doggedness: he moves back into the apartment, resumes the activities of daily life, cooks broccoli, bathes. Much of the time, it seems, he can't even look at the presence he's living with, but he can't leave it either: "Sat by his side every night averting my eyes from his hungry motheaten face," the poem says. This is the way the ancient Greeks knew the god of the underworld, Hades—his image appears on many vase paintings looking away, not only because it is impossible for the living to meet directly the gaze of death but because a hiddenness is fundamental to its nature.

So the trick, and it is a trick, is to let the lion into the house and not lose your allegiance to the world of the living—to live amid the overpowering knowledge and not allow it to drag you entirely into its realm. This is the poet as Scheherazade, acceding to her fate and yet delaying it by means of abundance and imagination, and by offering the cruel king the one thing he cannot do without: a story worth hearing. There lies one of the great source-springs of poetic power.

Some of you, scanning your own inner anthologies, may have already thought of another twentieth-century poem in the genre, one which speaks to a different possibility. Rilke's "The Panther" describes what happens if the vow is refused. The panther, pacing endlessly behind the bars of the Jardin des Plantes in Paris, seeing nothing except those bars, is finally brought to a kind of numbness and paralysis into which the entire world is swallowed. This is the fate also of the human spirit if, instead of acknowledging the impulse to give the self over, it tries to make of the untameable a thing caged.

The other danger, of course, is not refusal of the lion but putting yourself too easily into its mouth, forgetting to love also the infinite stories of the world. This might describe what happened to Sylvia Plath at the end of her life, in the blossoming of a strange serenity that enters the last poems. In the first line of one, "Edge," she eerily echoes Yeats's language in "The Choice": "the woman is perfected," she writes. Here, perfection (of the work? of the life?) is the vision of her own body composed in death, her two children coiled by her breasts. And in "Ariel," whose title refers not to Shakespeare's spirit-creation in "The Tempest" but to Plath's horse (named after that spirit), it's worth noticing how she describes the being whose fierce gallop leads her away from the dilemma of the world's claims and toward suicidal union: "God's lioness."

This too is a choice in dealing with the lion: to surrender. But thinking again of Ginsberg returning to the apartment and beginning to cook, I am reminded of another poem that begins with riding toward death, a meditation on courage and dailiness, Jack Gilbert's "The Abnormal is not Courage." In this poem, Gilbert speaks of the "magnitude of beauty" of the Polish cavalry who, at the beginning of World War II, rode directly into the guns of German tanks; still, he suggests, such "marvelous acts" are not in the end what courage is about. He offers instead the model of "even loyalty" to be found in a Penelope: "the marriage, / not the month's rapture. Not the exception. The beauty / that is of many days. Steady and clear . . . / the normal excellence, of long accomplishment."

To see persistence and the daily as itself the culmination is to live in the world of the living, which, as Gilbert points out, is braver even than going open-eyed to your death. And make no mistake—to give yourself fully to living is as hard as to give yourself to the lion. Most of us live most of the time in some duller, safer middle ground, feeling neither our terrors nor our joys—and the two are linked. It is no accident that one of the laws of poetry seems to be that there can be no good poem of unalloyed happiness, that good poems always pull in two directions, live in paradox and tension, as love poems, for example, live best in the knowledge of love's transience. This is also a law of the self: "Every angel is terrifying," Rilke told us. And so, if you are going to describe joy, perhaps it too must bring with it a shadow.

To look at how this works, here is a poem that seems to describe a moment of pure light, pure redemption, by Czeslaw Milosz (translated by Milosz):

GIFT

A day so happy.
Fog lifted early, I worked in the garden.
Hummingbirds were stopping over honeysuckle flowers.
There was no thing on earth I wanted to possess.
I knew no one worth my envying him.
Whatever evil I had suffered, I forgot.
To think that once I was the same man did not embarrass me.
In my body I felt no pain.
When straightening up, I saw the blue sea and sails.

Because we feel immediately that this is a good poem, we know it must have in its craftiness some part of the shadow—a lion who may be mostly hidden, but nonetheless present. The prestidigitation is done, I think, in two ways. The first is that in each outer thing named in the poem we recognize fleetingness and temporality—what could be more ephemeral than lifting fog, more quick than the unmentioned wings of the hummingbirds stopped above their flowers? Blue seas alter in a moment, raised sails are by definition passing us by. With the part of ourselves that reads the deep poem surrounding the poem that is at first apparent, we know that the entire scene is only an instant's reprieve from each of the things which form the second part of the trick, which is the part accom-plished through the rhetorical device of including something by putting it in the negative. Evil, suffering, physical pain, shame, the desire to possess—by telling us that for this moment each was forgotten, the poet makes us feel their presence pressing in upon him all around this moment. And it is this surrounding landscape of difficulty that gives to the poem's one day of peace its deep poignance. The title contributes as well: a gift is something unearned, unpurchasable, and so it is also something that cannot be controlled. In that thought, too, is the footprint of the lion.

Similarly, the best strategy for writing about horror may sometimes mean turning to horror's shadow-side: the fragile, yet persistent beauty of the world. One example of this is Frost's chilling war-sonnet, "Range-Finding":

> The battle rent a cobweb diamond-strung
> And cut a flower beside a ground bird's nest
> Before it stained a single human breast.
> The stricken flower bent double and so hung.
> And still the bird revisited her young.
> A butterfly its fall had dispossessed
> A moment sought in air his flower of rest,
> Then lightly stooped to it and fluttering clung.
>
> On the bare upland pasture there had spread
> O'ernight 'twixt mullein stalks a wheel of thread
> And straining cables wet with silver dew.
> A sudden passing bullet shook it dry.
> The indwelling spider ran to greet the fly,
> But finding nothing, sullenly withdrew.

This is the rhetoric of inclusion by denial taken to the next degree, where the thing actually being looked at in the poem goes almost completely unspoken—and this poem, I think, would be even better if Frost had trusted his readers more and left out the third line ("Before it stained a single human breast") completely. No mention of the human beyond the title is necessary for "Range-Finding" to make its point, and its point is chilling precisely because what is not included is the human carnage about to commence. The bent flower still holds its butterfly, the nestlings still live, even the shaken spiderweb is intact—by naming the litany of fragile things that survive the setting of the guns' scopes and aim, Frost leaves us to imagine everything else. And the fly of the final couplet, whose mention carries all the resonance of carrion death—fly as food for the spider; fly as what remains, feasting on, after the battle is over—is itself in fact an absence, a mistaken idea of the spider whose web has been brushed by a bullet. This poem is a kind of tour-de-force, its substance *all* held in shadow.

In his *Kadenshō*, a fifteenth-century teaching treatise on the development of an actor in Japanese Nō drama, Zeami (the foremost playwright and theoretician of Nō) describes the quality of the actor's highest art in terms of *hana*, flower. This flower is a kind of resonance or fragrance, an ineffable quality that radiates through the being of the actor and is the source of his greatness. In youth, Zeami admits, such *hana* may appear naturally, but in age it can only arise in the being of a thoroughly ripened person. And the central secret of mature *hana*, Zeami reveals at one point, is that it is itself the reflection of a secret, of knowledge withheld: the actor knows more than he shows. *Hana* is the result of the actor's own long reflection on human character and action, the culmination of not only training and technique but also of the development of his own mind. Yet none of this is displayed overtly, and Zeami cautions that even the fact that the actor possesses a secret should be kept secret. In another treatise he describes the highest stage of *hana* with a traditional Zen phrase, as being like "the light of the sun at midnight"—the presence of the flowering felt, paradoxically, most deeply in its utter absence.

Certain poems, like Milosz's "The Gift," have this quality as well—a perfection that has to do not with perfection in the overt sense of embodying some recognizable ideal but in the root sense of the word, meaning something which is thoroughly done. In even the simplest of such poems, a complexity hovers, sign of a consciousness which has been developed by long consideration, long encounter with many things. Such poems have a shadow because they have being, substance, history, inescapably within what they see and what they know and how they convey that to us. They know more than they tell us. They keep secrets. Yet those unspoken aspects of the poem shape and flavor and alter what is said.

An odd thought rises to mind about this, a thought relating to shadow's role in poetry in the more conventional Jungian sense of shadow as the side of the self with which we are most uncomfortable. It is a way to begin to think about a phenomenon much discussed recently, after the publication of Philip Larkin's letters: how is it that again and again we find that some of the poems we most love and admire were written by people whose character we can most kindly describe as deeply flawed? It is the question not only of Larkin's misogyny and bigotry but also of Stevens's racism and Pound's and Eliot's anti-Semitism and the deep streak of cruelty found in the lives of all too many of the leading poets of the twentieth century. In a letter to Harry Chambers, Larkin himself said, "I've always taken comfort from D. H. L[awrence]'s 'You have to have something vicious in you to be a creative writer.'"

My thought is this—perhaps the bitterness, vanity, selfishness, and fear that are to one extent or another part of all of our characters may in fact give a flavor of the shadow's complexity to those poems which are forced to struggle particularly hard against them. Perhaps a cruel eye, if kept in check well enough by the even fiercer demands of making good art, may at least at times make for a better poet than a lazy eye or a stupid or sleeping one, or one that willingly blinds itself to the more harsh aspects of the world and the human. A poem that struggles against its own bitterness may seem gallant, but one that struggles against the saccharin will be merely pitiful. I discussed this with one friend, the poet Kay Ryan, and she came up with an interesting phrase—"Yes," she said, "it's as if such poets are holding a knife by the blade while they write." And so, in the attempt to cut neither the reader nor themselves, an astonishing tenderness and even compassion may emerge.

For there is no question that the best of Larkin's poems move finally toward a tenderness, born perhaps out of knowing the wound of a sharp judgment turned as quickly upon himself as it was outward. In such poems, as soon as he begins to judge, as soon as the edge of bitterness rises, Larkin widens the perspective, includes himself, and the poem steps into something else. You can see the same gesture at work in two of his best known poems, "This Be The Verse" and "High Windows." In the latter example, there's no missing the bitterness Larkin feels (probably with good cause, given what we know of his life) about his own disordered sex life and lost opportunities, but then the poem moves from anger to something completely mysterious, the image of openness to light and air with which it ends. The way he accomplishes this is a point of craft that cannot be learned except in the heart itself—it cannot be faked or cobbled together the way a good simile can at times be cobbled together. We may learn it from our own lives, or we may possibly be able to learn it from reading, but eventually part of a person's ripening means not excusing oneself anymore. Larkin at his best doesn't let Larkin at his worst off the hook, nor does he avoid Larkin at his worst. He does the one thing he is able to do: he lives with him as best he can, and he looks at it all.

The ability to hold the worse parts of the self as also subject to examination and judgment may also (and I know some would disagree) redeem Robert Lowell from disaster; redeem him, for example, for the sonnets he wrote about the end of his marriage to Elizabeth Hardwick. Here is the poem I have in mind—

DOLPHIN

My Dolphin, you only guide me by surprise,
captive as Racine, the man of craft,
drawn through his maze of iron composition
by the incomparable wandering voice of Phedre.
When I was troubled in mind, you made for my body
caught in its hangman's-knot of sinking lines,
the glassy bowing and scraping of my will . . .
I have sat and listened to too many
words of the collaborating muse,
and plotted perhaps too freely with my life,
not avoiding injury to others,
not avoiding injury to myself—
to ask compassion . . . this book, half fiction,
an eelnet made by man for the eel fighting—

my eyes have seen what my hand did.

I'll be returning to this poem later, but it's worth noticing that its imagery goes all the way back to Lowell's first book, where "The Quaker Graveyard in Nantucket" opens with the image of a drowned sailor clutching a drag-net and closes with the line, "The Lord survives the rainbow of his will." A lifetime later, the poet is still working the same vein of ore, still pondering the body drowned in the web of the world and how it got there. By the very fact of his admitting complicity and refusing to ask forgiveness he wins—from this reader at least—what he knows he cannot ask: our compassion and pity even for his cruelty.

In Catholic mysticism, there is a path known as the *via negativa*. This refers to the practice of emptying the self, the soul, of its own will, desires, and even knowledge, in order that it can then be filled by God. A similar path can be found at work in poetry, in several guises. The first place we find it is in the relationship between speech and its shadow side, silence, that many poets have described. The voice of the poem often does not arise except from a prior silence of being, and in order to speak at all many writers have devised ways of inviting this silence first to enter their minds, whether or not they recognize the process for what it is. The small rituals preceding writing—Flaubert's drawer of rotting apples opened and smelled, the sharpening of pencils, the contemplative cup of tea—all are ways of removing the mind from the quotidian and turning toward the concentration of writing. By interrupting the flow of thoughts concerned with errands, chores, daily relationships, and so on, a deeper kind of thinking and a different music of thought find room to surface—and this is so even if the eventual poem is one which speaks of errands, chores, and daily relationships; otherwise, any of us could just as well write the poems of James Schuyler or John Ashbery, by an act of simple transcription.

Silence can be frightening to a writer, and yet the passage through silence is a necessary part of the way into words. The fear is fear of the unknown—it reminds us of the old maps on which unexplored places were marked, "In this place there be dragons." Yet leaving the safety of the known and stepping into the uncharted terrain for which we do not yet have words is the only way to begin to say something real, whether about the shadow-self or about groceries. This brings us to the second place that we find the *via negativa* in the making of poems: Keats's conception of Negative Capability, the ability of the writer to abide in the realm of mystery and uncertainty, free of any "irritable reaching after facts." In another of his letters, Keats says of the poet's character that "it is not itself—it has no self—it is every thing and nothing—" and, using language that comes straight from the mystics, he speaks of the self as being "annihilated" by all that presses in around it. The writer following this path gives him- or herself over not only to the imagination and its works, but to the world itself.

There is another "negative way" in poetry as well—the actual use of the negative, as we glimpsed earlier in Milosz's "Gift." I have begun to look at how often such explicit negative constructions appear in poems I love, how often they occur at a poem's turning point, freeing the poet to move a stage deeper into his or her own being and saying. It is a way of stepping by means of grammar into the unknown and into the shadow-realm, to see what gifts that place of not-knowing may offer.

One of the great practitioners of this use of the negative is a poet we often think of as one of our most luminous, James Wright, and I strongly suspect that these two aspects of his work are related. Especially in the later work, which is filled with a tenderness and compassion unsurpassed in contemporary poetry, such phrases recur with enormous frequency. In writing this piece, I opened randomly the posthumous collection *This Journey*, published two years after Wright's death in 1980, and there could not be a better example than the poem I found, one about Saint Jerome.

Before giving it, I'll pause to note that Wright's fascination with saints goes back at least to his second book, *Saint Judas*. It may also help to know a little about Jerome. He lived from roughly 342 to 420, and was not only made a saint but also given the rarer title of "doctor of the church" for his work as both theologian and translator. After a long period of fierce engagement and controversy over church affairs, he retired for many years to a desert monastic community near Bethlehem, where he completed a translation from the Hebrew of the Old Testament. It's during this time of late respite that the poem is set.

Jerome in Solitude

To see the lizard there,
I was amazed I did not have to beat
My breast with a stone.

If a lion lounged nearby,
He must have curled in a shadow of cypress,
For nobody shook a snarled mane and stretched out
To lie at my feet.

And, for a moment,
I did not see Christ retching in pain, longing

To clutch his cold abdomen,
Sagging, unable to rise or fall, the human
Flesh torn between air and air.

I was not even
Praying, unless: no,
I was not praying.

A rust branch fell suddenly
Down from a dead cypress
And blazed gold. I leaned close.
The deep place in the lizard's eye
Looked back into me.

Delicate green sheaths
Folded into one another.
The lizard was alive,
Happy to move.

But he did not move.
Neither did I.
I did not dare to.

I scarcely know where to begin talking about this poem, except by swearing I really did open the book at random. I did not look for a poem with a lion in it—yet there one was, present through the strategy of claiming his absence. He is, interestingly, "curled in a shadow," and from that place of peaceable acknowledgment, I think, blesses the poem, the saint, the poet. (The lion, by the way, is the companion-animal of Saint Jerome, appearing at rest near his feet in the many paintings of Jerome at work at his desk.)

Next, I notice how each of the first four stanzas progresses by means of statements in the negative. "I did not have to beat / My breast with a stone." "Nobody shook a snarled mane and stretched out / To lie at my feet." "And for a moment, I did not see Christ retching in pain, longing to clutch his cold abdomen . . ." (In these lines you can see how powerfully Wright's use of the negative allows the image that follows it to enter us— by pretending to release us from the vision of Christ's all-too-human agony, he in fact includes us in it.) And finally, "I was not even / Praying, unless: no, / I was not praying." The negative statement, the reconsidering pause, the repetition, even more definitive—and yet, instead of closing the poem down, the gesture opens it up for the moment of the psyche's deepening and epiphany: there is the blazing gold of what at first appears to be a fallen branch, there is the "deep place in the lizard's eye" looking back "into" the poet. The lizard is small and seemingly inconsequential, as virtually all of James Wright's messenger angels are, and yet his mere being is a gate entered not by suffering, but as the pure gift that can arise when we are doing nothing, if we are doing nothing deeply enough.

It is a deeper enactment of the thought from that earlier poem of Wright's, "Saint Judas." In that sonnet, Judas, going off to kill himself after the crucifixion, is stopped by the sight of a man being beaten by hoodlums—he drops the rope with which he intends to hang himself, runs unthinkingly and without any consciousness of self to the victim "beaten, / Stripped, kneed, and left to cry," and

> Then I remembered bread my flesh had eaten,
> The kiss that ate my flesh. Flayed without hope,
> I held the man for nothing in my arms.

Only in that nothing can a gift be given or received. It is, I believe, the pursuit through dark poem after dark poem of that nothing, the state when a person passes beyond valuation and evaluation and becomes only himself, that led Wright from the bitter residues of his Depression-era childhood and early breakdown and subsequent alcoholism to the redemption and—there is no other word for it—grace of the late work. Throughout his life as a writer he wrote of the lost souls, the ones fallen into the river and destroyed; throughout his life as a writer he was willing to follow them into those places of raging in the dark. And still we find him at the end of "Jerome in Solitude" (which must be, whether consciously or unconsciously, a self-portrait) in a moment of pure suspension, deep in the great happiness of being alive in the saint, in the delicate green folds of the lizard's skin, in the held breath of amazement at the existence of life itself. Surely there is a connection.

Both "The Gift" and "Jerome in Solitude" show us a grace which occurs as a moment both embedded in and removed from the flux of world and time. I do not think that it is an accident that both poems use what I have called the "negative way" to achieve their separate miracles—these are rare poems, poems which in fact do manage to realize for us an image, however precarious and fleeting, of what the heavenly mansion looks like. It looks like sailboats on blue water, it looks like the eye of a lizard. Yet the only path to such a poem is the willingness to include its opposite, to live as long as is necessary raging in the dark, not attempting to turn away, not attempting to exclude the difficult part of our knowledge of what the world is.

And so I'd like to finish by going back to Lowell's "Dolphin," a poem caught on the verge, perhaps, of grace—a poem that shows us how a poet moves (though perhaps deliberately, given Lowell's superb use of sound throughout his career) clumsily, awkwardly, unmusically, apologetically, toward it. The dolphin—Lowell's version of the untameable spirit-animal of redemption—comes, if it comes, not by any act the poet can control but only by surprise and as gift, to rescue the person who knows himself drowning in a hangman's net of his own construction, result of his human and fallible will. "My eyes have seen what my hand did," the poem concludes, neither excusing nor blaming. The statement is not only an acknowledgment and a description, but also offers, I think, a possible direction: this is a course we can attempt, in our own clumsy navigation of the shadow in world and in self.

We cannot control the dolphin, or the lion, or the gift that comes to us as a single day of grace. We cannot choose whether or not we will be ready to throw ourselves over the ledge to where the starving tiger looks up. What we can do is be willing to see what we do, what we are, what we find around us, and to stake our claim in the marriage of craft to that unflinching, steadfast looking. We can write the truth. We can approach it from every side: above, below, backward. We can follow our own obsessions and images over the course of a lifetime, returning and returning to the body knotted in its ropes in the sea at the center of our grief. Yeats's choice, I think, is a false dichotomy: raging in the dark is the way to the heavenly mansion, whether in the work or in the life. We have the task clearly before us—as Lowell put it elsewhere, in a line I have come to love in a way free of the circumstances of its writing, "Why not say what happened?" If the thought is interpreted deeply and widely enough, with freedom and grace, and if we are willing to live with the lion, the tiger, the wild and unbeckonable dolphin we dare not even hope for—something unknowable may come of such a path. It is a way. It will do.

DAVID RIVARD

Paint Brushes vs. Rollers: On Class Warfare, Honor, and the Cosmos

[INDIANA UNIVERSITY WRITERS' CONFERENCE]

I bought a house last year. I bought a house, and, as the soldier who narrates Frank O'Connor's "Guests of the Nation" says, "anything that ever happened me after I never felt the same about again." And nothing that ever happened me before either.

There's nothing out of the ordinary with somebody buying a house in America, except that I had never figured on doing it—but there I was, flush with money from a writing grant, enough for a down-payment in a real estate market that had crashed. My wife and I were signing the papers, *closing*, moving on up into a three-story Victorian in a middle-class neighborhood near Harvard. Before we could move in though the house would need some work. We contracted out the bigger projects—a new roof and porches, a kitchen rehab—but wanted to do the rest ourselves, some demolition, a little plastering, a lot of painting. My father offered his help.

My father, a retired firefighter who had worked on the side as a painting contractor, spent most of his adult life painting houses. Both of his jobs were full time, and so he had mostly been an absent presence around our home as I grew up. I had worked for him myself a couple of years during my teens, years when we were often at odds as I looked for a one-way ticket out of Fall River, the Massachusetts mill town where I was born. Since then, I'd lived in Boston and Stockholm and Princeton and Tucson and San Francisco. With no exaggeration I can say we'd spent hardly more than two or three hours alone together at a time since I'd left. Now he was driving up to Cambridge every day, and we were working side by side, repairing window sashes, stripping wallpaper, spackling, puttying, caulking, sanding, priming . . . and arguing.

One morning, as I headed out the door to a local paint shop, I mentioned that I intended to buy some rollers so we could start painting the ceilings. Wait, he said, hadn't he told me we would use *only* brushes on this job? I'd thought he was kidding, or that at least he wouldn't dig in stubbornly against something it seemed obvious would make the job go faster. I should have known better. I should have remembered how he'd started out in the late '40s as an apprentice in a painters' union local, a shop in which the journeymen had actually worn white shirts and ties when they worked; and how compulsively meticulous a craftsman he'd been (an annoying perfectionist to my distracted and bored teenage slacker). I should have recalled the pride that had always seemed to border on righteous indignation, a mix of gruff assurance and defensiveness. This was really a fight about authority. Who had more authority, and who, therefore, could speak, who could say what must be done.

As the fight escalated, it sounded as if we were talking two different languages, the tongues of long-suspicious tribes with discordant experiences and memories. As often happens when people speak mutually incomprehensible languages, we got louder and louder trying to make ourselves understood (that is, attempting to convince each other of our rightness). I remember my father angrily accusing me of having no respect for the forty years he'd painted. I asked him not to treat me like an idiot child. And so on. Rollers versus brushes might as well have represented competing ways of seeing the cosmos. Not just of seeing it, but of speaking of it. Then, after we'd exhausted ourselves and shut it down, I ended up stomping out of the house and driving around for hours. Just like the old days.

When poets, across time, speak of the language of their art . . . they speak of it as a dialect, or the language of a class: W. C. Williams speaks not his own speech but the "American idiom"; Wordsworth aspires to speak in the language of the lower and middle classes, as we learn from his "Preface"; Yeats undertook to speak in the language of the archetypes—the dead, the heroes on the wind, the historical aristocracy, both divine and human; Shakespeare spoke in the language of his social betters, the language of the aristocracy of his time. *Each poet chooses not the language of an individual but the language of a class—for reasons.* Among those reasons are that . . . the language of a class has the immortality of a community and the extended reference of horizon of a community, and also, what is more important, inside it the sanctions and authenticity of a community derived from the same sources that make the world possible . . .

This is Allen Grossman, from *The Sighted Singer*, a wonderful collection of conversations with his former student, the poet Mark Halliday. I have two reactions to this statement. First, its air of heroic intelligence and *pronunciamento* makes me want to nod my head in agreement, as if it were simply common sense. What Grossman says here *is* true. How could it not be? But I think Allen Grossman gets it only partly right.

The class that I have chosen for my voice does not resemble anything as monolithic or stable or uniform as Grossman's statement implies—in fact, my voice sounds as if made up of many different classes (in the same way that a poem can be polyphonic or multitonal). At its heart, though, is an on-going "betrayal" of the voice of my original class: my father's voice, if you want to call it that. But this betrayal, paradoxically, keeps me returning to a working-class consciousness, tethered to the language from which I came, because the moment of betrayal demands a counterbalance, a loyalty, which, once enacted, must be abandoned in turn. That restless oscillation strikes me as the source and method for much of my work, as well as a version of the primal American poetic experience, from Whitman ("I too lived, Brooklyn of ample hills was mine, / . . . I too had been struck from the float held forever in solution") on down to Ashbery ("I tried many things, only some were immortal and free"). Abandonment and loyalty in the remaking of the self.

I wasn't supposed to write poetry. My family owned few books—a set of the *World Book* encyclopedia, pulp thrillers, catalogs and almanacs, popular magazines—certainly no volume of poems, no anthology. For me, poetry was the horrible patriotic "verse" the Sisters of Mercy forced us to write on the blackboard as a punishment during grammar school detention sessions. No early and fated brush with Keats or Dickinson or Frost inspired me. My grandfather did not correspond in verse with the local

bank president, as Pound's did. No one encouraged me to be "creative."
My family's ambitions for me were those of the aspiring working class:
that I become a lawyer or doctor or accountant, I suppose, and that I enter
the world of comforts and professional attainment denied my parents.

Something happened. The arc of the story is a pretty typical version of
my generation's jihad, and it goes something like this: New Left politics
to drugs to rock 'n' roll to anthropology to poetry. Or Abbie Hoffman to
chocolate mescaline to Dylan to shamanism to Merwin. And the story beneath the story is about my wanting to escape, from my family, from the
granite mills and the lousy jobs, from the gloomy French-Canadian and
Portuguese Catholicism. When I finally started reading poetry late in college, the poets I loved had nothing to do with the place where I grew up.
Reading Stevens and Charles Olson and Gary Snyder and Berryman was
like dropping a full hit of whatever was *other*. In the early '70s, I listened
to Merwin and Adrienne Rich read at an old Baptist church in Providence, and was knocked out. Weirdly enough, because I loved what I
heard, I felt I could actually do it myself, I could speak that way. As with
most forms of love, something absolutely other was made to seem absolutely real, already nearly possessed by me, already possessing me. Another language seemed immediately possible.

I first loved poetry because it wasn't like anything I'd ever heard before
(or so I thought). Even when I hooked onto someone like Richard Hugo,
I hardly noticed how his West, with its caved-in mining towns and struggling citizens, strangely echoed what I was familiar with at home—I cared
more about his sound, the odd syntax and turns of phrase, the peculiar images and rhythms. I didn't know it then but I was in love with music, and
with metaphor, its root in the Greek meaning "to carry, transport."

But building the chassis for my own little poetic go-cart, even checking
out the high-priced models at the dealerships down the road, all this involved a betrayal, one that was both pleasurable and guilt-laden. I was doing something that had no place in the community from which I came. No
standing in the pragmatic world of shop stewards and cops and tillermen.
So there seemed no use in calling attention to myself. I hardly spoke of it
with my family, never called myself a poet (I said vaguely that I was interested in "writing").

The language of my early poems was dense and manically figured, so
encoded into metaphor that it was impossible to know what I was writing

about (I doubt that I knew, and I can't imagine how anyone else would have). This feverish language, it had some odd sources. Partly my natural shyness, as well as the reticence typical of many when they start to write about their lives. Partly my desire to divorce myself from the common language, the words of my birthplace. Partly as a way of both disguising and overcoming my insecurities about being a poet (as if I could prove my right to use poetic language *only* by using it in an exaggerated manner). And partly for the true pleasure that it is. I loved the ways in which words surprised. I understood almost immediately how poetry is a form of subversive play, and delight, even at its darkest or most earnest. I needed it. And I saw how that playfulness and impracticality might make it seem both foolish and a threat.

The capacious pleasure of throwing words together, of making what Hugo considers "private" language, has for me always been tinged by an odd guilt. Not simply that I'm doing something that is alien to my original community, that has small sanction there, but also that I do something more traditionally associated with the upper classes, with privilege. It was as if, in writing a poem, I double-crossed those closest to me. In a way, too, I still imagine myself as a usurper, a spy under the mill-owner's son's bed, an impersonator who has stolen a privilege to wear poetry, as if it were a frock coat. I like having gotten away with it, with making the coat mine, but it doesn't always feel comfortable (nor should it necessarily). I have to keep making the right mine, it hasn't come to me by birth. And just because I've claimed the right, that doesn't mean I've been admitted to the class which has traditionally owned it.

In truth, I'm shadowed by the class from which I came. I am not liberated from it, haven't transcended it. The language of that class hasn't been suppressed in my work. It is both transformed and untransformable. After I had written poems for a few years, the language and experience of Fall River started creeping back into my work, just when I began to try and figure out what it was that I was writing about. When I had to see who I could be in my poems (not just who I had been or was, but who I *could be*), I went back to my first mirror. When I needed to discover my self in my poems I returned to my first language, a language that for a long time had hardly sounded "poetic" at all.

It was at that point that I became aware of how ambivalent my sense of the privilege of poetry was. Some of this ambivalence has to do with seeing class conflict in terms other than those of money or material power. Allen Grossman pins it down beautifully in *The Sighted Singer*:

> . . . conflict between classes in America seems very specifically to be conflict gener-
> ated by deprivation not of wealth but of honor, the designed scarcity of the privilege
> of acknowledgement. . . .

When I started writing more directly, openly, about my experience, I felt this deficit of honor and acknowledgment. I wasn't sure my words counted. Was I writing poetry? How could the language of Fall River be made into poems? I wasn't sure it was possible. The poetry I was attracted to, my models, started to change. Levine became immensely important, along with James Wright, Dugan. Looking for ways to shape idiom into poetry, I went to Frost and Hardy, to Robinson and William Carlos Williams. But every time I settled down to work, my doubts sat down with me.

When I had left grad school at Princeton, where I'd been studying anthropology and sneaking writing courses on the sly with Ted Weiss, and then later when I moved to Arizona to start an M.F.A. in poetry, my parents had been bitterly disappointed, my father especially. For a long time a great gap remained between us. When my writing started to change, when I started writing about the people and place of Fall River, I may have been trying to speak to them again, in the language of our tribe. But I always felt divided against that language by the fact of making it into poetry, by transforming it, by "using" it in certain ways; all without being sure I had the authority to attempt that transformation.

In looking for authority, for a source, and unconscious of the needs driving it, I did what was natural: I went back to my primal experience of authority, my father. To put this another way, I remember my friend, the fiction writer Peter Behrens, telling me in 1984 that it was our job to write our father's stories. But those stories had as much to do with a *way* of telling as with specific events. In my first book of poems, *Torque*, only three poems deal directly with my father's life and character, while one other mentions him in a fairly casual way—yet the book is illuminated by his speech, even when he is not speaking or being spoken about. This was brought home to me after he read the book and, having asked me if I was at work on another, half-jokingly requested that I leave him out of the next one. He said this at my grandmother's wake, a fact that naturally amplified both the cutting humor and the disturbing adamancy of the remark. At first I thought he was merely being ironically appreciative (typical of my father to voice his pride in such an inverted manner!). Either that, or pretty egotistical and off the wall, since the book contained thirty-one other poems having nothing to do with him. Then I had one of those kinds of insights that seem hallucinatory because so convincingly sudden: that he had intuited the degree to which my poems depended on his manner of speaking, and on his attitudes toward experience. Perhaps it would be more accurate to say that *I* understood this for the first time.

Half-consciously, I had created a voice (and by necessity a speaker, an identity, a self with all its variance of character) that tapped my father's authority. In my poems, I had chosen to be a certain type of man (the type that had been a model for my father as well). As Allen Grossman says, ". . . each poet chooses not the language of an individual but the language of a class. . . ."

It's useful here to give an example, from *Torque*, of what I'm talking about. This is the title poem:

> After his ham & cheese in the drape factory cafeteria,
> having slipped by the bald shipping foreman
> to ride a rattling elevator to the attic
> where doves flicker into the massive eaves
> and where piled boxes of out-of-style
> cotton and lace won't ever be
> decorating anyone's sun parlor windows.
> Having dozed off in that hideout he fixed
> between five four-by-six cardboard storage cartons
> while the rest of us pack Mediterranean Dreams
> and Colonial Ruffles and drapes colored like moons,
> and he wakes lost—
> shot through
> into a world of unlocked unlocking light—
> suddenly he knows where he is and feels half nuts
> and feels like killing some pigeons with a slingshot.

> That's all, and that's why he pokes
> his calloused fingers into broken machinery,
> hunting for loose nuts a half-inch wide—
> five greasy cold ones that warm in his pocket—
> and yanks back the snag-cut strip of inner tube
> with a nut snug at the curve to snap it
> at the soft chest of a dopey bird.
> Then the noise of pigeons flopping down
> to creosoted hardwood, and then a grin
> the guy gives me & all his other pals later.
> And afternoon tightens down on all
> our shoulders, until the shift whistle
> blasts, blowing through the plant like air
> through lace. As it always has, as it does.
> That bright. That stunned.

If this poem is the product of a working-class consciousness, then I think it illustrates the point in more ways than subject or setting. For one thing, I hear in its dominant tone a kind of assurance, almost an arrogance, that belies the situation of the speaker and his fellow workers (a lousy job in a textile mill, and the moment of mindless cruelty it seems to provoke)—it's as if that assurance, with its ironies and tough-guy grin and name-calling ("dopey bird"), could hold off the forces that threaten it. This is a matter, as it should be, of endurance. To seem more vulnerable or "sensitive" would be to admit defeat.

I come from a place that has been struggling, suffering, for a long time. Fall River looks demographically more like a pocket of Appalachian poverty, with chronically high unemployment and dropout rates, sweat shops paying low wages, health problems—a place that never really recovered from the Depression of the '30s (before which it had been a cotton manufacturing capital), and that, in terms of its culture, might as well be five hundred as opposed to fifty miles from Boston. But, in the people who live there, now a predominantly immigrant community of Azorean Portuguese, there is a resistance to defeat, though it often finds its expression in distorted ways, largely in a cynical fatalism that poses as a knowledge of life, in an unsentimental, assertive "attitude." You can hear this in various lines: "where piled boxes of out-of-style / cotton and lace won't ever be / decorating anyone's sun parlor windows" or "That's all, and that's why he pokes" or "As it always has, as it does." This attitude is what remains when so much has been taken away. You may be deprived of honor, but you don't have to be a fool.

You don't have to be a fool. One of the great values given me by my father, by the men I grew up among, was the hatred of privilege. A sense of outrage, not at being down, but at someone having an advantage over you and seeming to be "better." In Fall River, this is as much a matter of geography as wealth or education or title—whereas the proverbial railroad tracks divide most towns, for us it was landscape, a granite ridge that bisects most of the city. My father grew up "below the hill," in one of the poorest wards, where my mother's father and grandfather had been beat cops. The triple-decker we lived in sat at the other end of the city, at the bottom of the city's steepest hill, Weetamoe Street. Above us, the section of town called The Highlands, where the factory owners and businessmen, the professional classes, had their homes. Privilege seemed the privilege to ignore, as much as anything else: not to see, and therefore to strip someone of their identity. It still seems this way to me. To be opposed to privilege is to have a sense of your own dignity, of your person. But in writing poems (maybe even in owning a house!), I have done something I implicitly equate with privilege, sensing it separates me from the people with whom I should belong. I feel self-divided. And perhaps I have always looked for ways to mend this division.

My father's fatalism—that mix of pessimism and cynical knowingness he inherited largely from my Quebeçois grandmother, who worked fifty years as a seamstress in the mills, a birthright that he then exercised daily in the male, barracks atmosphere of the firehouse—this fatalism was something I took up instinctively. I can hear it in "Torque," and throughout my book. In order to feel seen, the speaker is at pains to say the "truth," no matter how terrible, in plain talk: "suddenly he knows where he is and feels half nuts." Then that perspective widens, taking up the encompassing scope implied by fatalism: "And afternoon tightens down on all / our shoulders. . . . As it always has, as it does" (this last phrase, it surely echoes the Catholic prayers I heard in church and school). This fatalism was immensely attractive as a source of authority, though at the time I didn't recognize the seductiveness of its anger and bitterness. Or maybe I did, but—proud, needing it—ignored the woundedness of this anger. It, and the arrogance it shaded into, may have enabled me to overcome my doubts about being a poet. It gave me a place and a people and a voice with which to identify, an identity.

Unfortunately, it also threatened to swallow up certain vulnerabilities, those parts of my character that had probably led me to poetry and that were different from those of the male working class in which I had been brought up. In other words, the voice didn't feel entirely comfortable; re-reading the poem now, I hear those other pieces of my character trying to disrupt it—and this attempted disruption causes a kind of tension in the language, a drama in the language, almost under its surface. I hear this in the flexing and unwinding of the sentences, and in the heightened, coun-terpointing music of lines like "and yanks back the snag-cut strip of inner tube / with a nut snug at the curve to snap it / at the soft chest of a dopey bird." And I sense how close the speaker is to identifying with that bird. And how, in the naming of the different styles of drapery or in the line "into a world of unlocked unlocking light," the speaker almost steps out of character—how longing, which can be opposed to fatalism, locates it-self in those lines. That is some kind of "otherness" asserting itself—whatever is not a part of the community and its dominant attitudes—in-terrupting, even if it is more or less *sub rosa*.

Czeslaw Milosz quotes Simone Weil as saying in one of her essays that "whoever tries to escape an inevitable contradiction by patching it up is a coward." I wouldn't go so far as to describe what I had done in my first book in adopting a voice that overrode the other voices in me as an act of cowardice—in many ways it allowed me to embrace a part of myself that I had ignored or denied, for better or worse, for a time. But there was something partial and limiting about the voice and its attitudes. Didn't I feel a great deal more tenderness or grief about things that had happened to me, or to my friends, my family? Wasn't there also a language that I used everyday, and that I had loved first as a teenager, that had more to do with philosophy and art? Wasn't I more naive in character than I allowed myself in my poems? What about humor and wit? What about the ways in which I *wasn't* a man like my father? What about the ways in which *he* wasn't?

As I finish my second book now, I'm not sure how much I've accom-plished of the work implied by these questions. Some. The voice in my new poems *is* different from the one in *Torque*. At least it points to a fluid-ity of identity. That fluidity seems possible because I have tried to amplify those contradictions of language and experience which I had previously dampened in the interest of authority. The sources of my authority are different, less singular than previously. The dominant fatalistic attitude is jimmied out of place more often. I have wanted to get a different kind of doubt into my poems, one based less on a fatalistic belief that the world is a terrible place than on an uncertainty that arises from the possibility that the self might be many things and that the world might contain many things in it in which to have faith. Hope might be possible, even when it was not.

I think that, before I finished *Torque*, my poems wanted to decide matters, to stay my confusion through a process of argument and judgment (both judgment of others and self-judgment). Now, I'm not sure they aren't still arguing with themselves, but they seem less inclined to resolve. The poems don't exactly conclude in the same ways. They want to accumulate, to increase the tension until something unexpected happens. They're tonally more varied, the pitch can alter suddenly. The voice "floats" more, with less narrative structure. Interestingly, my models for this kind of voice have been distant ones, largely poets from central Europe: Milosz, Herbert, Adam Zagajewski, Tomaz Salamun. I identify with the sense of displacement Milosz talks about, and with how he implies exile can often be a gift, not simply a burden:

> I have been tossed by circumstances, from one civilization into another, from high-pressure areas into low, and vice-versa. From the Russian Revolution of 1917 seen through the eyes of a child and a foreigner, to New Mexico and California, all the way to the old house on Lake Geneva, I have wandered through zones of storm and calm, heat and cold. New images cancelled out none of the old, and, strictly speaking, I do not see them in chronological order as if on a strip of film, but in parallel, colliding with one another, overlapping.

What Milosz says about images—about the ways new ones do not cancel out old, about their lack of linearity, and their tendencies to collide—might just as easily be said about diction, tone, syntactical phrasings, metaphors. For me, the restlessness such collisions reflect has as much to do with movement across classes as it does with physical uprooting or travel. I have come to accept it. It might have been that, early on, I didn't feel myself sufficiently a part of "the Tradition" to speak. If so, that has not, ultimately, been a terrible thing. I wanted badly enough to use the idiom of my home, in order to prove it as poetry (so it would be seen and heard), and perhaps to prove my loyalty as well; just as I wished to use the language of "poetry" to prove myself *other* than what I was. Loyalty and abandonment. These impulses continue their warfare. There are places to stand, but only temporarily. Perhaps I'm a visitor through the classes, an outsider to them all. This is another kind of privilege. It is a little like a conversation with my father, the ones where we don't have to yell at each other.

Zapata's Disciple and Perfect Brie

In December 1950, in Biloxi, Mississippi, my father was arrested for not going to the back of the bus. A dark-skinned Puerto Rican raised in New York, he had not learned to accept the laws of Jim Crow. A judge sentenced him to a week in jail, wiping out his Christmas furlough from the Air Force. This is what he learned: (1) he would be branded for the rest of his life by the brown pigment of his skin, and (2) he would fight. He would rather sit in jail than at the back of the bus.

My father's social class was defined by the opportunities denied him because of racism, and the opportunities he created for himself in spite of racism; the assignment of a servile status based on skin color, and his furious rejection of that status, for himself and others. His experiences — the frustrations and rages, the stubborn resistance, the dignity of his defiance — formed the environment in which I evolved, as son and poet, contributing to my awareness of class and its punishments.

What most damaged my father was the lack of a college education. Instead, there was a succession of jobs and places. Mechanic in the Air Force, a training he was not permitted to use as a civilian. A grocery store, which he abandoned after pulling a gun on thugs demanding protection money. Semiprofessional baseball. A sanitation crew cleaning the Holland Tunnel in New York, where he fell off a truck and injured his back. There may have been music somewhere: A family legend tells of drums sold to pay the rent. Or writing: A typewriter, hocked many times, didn't come back one day. When I was born, in 1957, he was working for an electrical contractor, and by all accounts hating it.

Political activism was his salvation. He began by organizing in his own community, the East New York section of Brooklyn. He organized rent strikes, voter registration drives, sit-ins of welfare mothers, marches for safe streets and civil rights. He was a fierce stump speaker, who once shared a podium at a rally with Malcolm X. He went to jail again. He was that most dangerous of creatures, a working-class radical. James Graham, in *The Enemies of the Poor*, compared my father to a guerrilla-disciple of Emiliano Zapata, the Mexican revolutionary.

He rose through the political ranks in New York City, directing a series of community-based organizations and programs. At the height of his influence as a leader, he walked away from the wars. He had always been a photographer, and in the late 1970s a grant enabled him to create the Puerto Rican Diaspora Documentary Project, a photodocumentary and oral history of the Puerto Rican migration across the United States. He is still a photographer today.

I spent my childhood in working-class housing projects in East New York. The projects were not yet the stereotypical swamps breeding a malaria of crime and drugs, but projects nevertheless, dreary institutional housing, the urban reservation meant to confine the urban savage. The environment was full of paranoia and tinged with violence: A grocer murdered in a robbery, a friend beaten and stripped by a local gang. Yet, in this environment, I was raised with an ethos of resistance all around me. Some of my earliest drawings depict demonstrations, sketched on the back of flyers announcing those same demonstrations. I remember, from the age of eight, a march and candlelight vigil for a short-order cook kicked to death by junkies, a spontaneous outpouring of grief and compassion burned so deeply into my imagination that I wrote a poem about it over twenty years later: "The Moon Shatters on Alabama Avenue."

As my father moved from blue-collar to white-collar work, our social status changed. We left the projects. However, being Puerto Rican in effect canceled out whatever middle-class trappings we had acquired for ourselves. In a Long Island high school, surrounded by the children of white flight, I faced racial obscenities everywhere, spray-painted on my locker and even scrawled in the icing on a cake. The brawls were inevitable: Being kicked repeatedly in a classroom while the teacher looked away, or having my head slammed into a water fountain. Here, the gangs were called fraternities.

Not coincidentally, at this time I began to write poetry, as an attempt to explain myself to myself. This writing, however, was not for the consumption of teachers, or for school. I was a spectacularly marginal student. In fact, I was so seriously alienated that I once failed English. I failed typing, too, but that was because I was tapping out poems instead of The Quick Brown Fox, etc.

In the recession of the 1970s and early 1980s, I wandered in and out of school, from job to job. This is my résumé: janitor at Sears, bindery worker in a printing plant, gas station attendant, door-to-door encyclopedia salesman, pizza cook, telephone solicitor, car washer for a factory showroom, bouncer in a bar, caretaker in a primate laboratory, night desk clerk in a transient hotel, worker on a cleaning crew for a minor league ballpark, radio journalist in Nicaragua, patient rights advocate in Wisconsin mental hospitals, and welfare rights paralegal, among others. I was not in the business of collecting colorful anecdotes; when I took a job, I was always in need of a job. Recently, an interviewer asked why I chose to work as a bouncer. Because I thought it would look good when I came up for tenure, I said.

Working was better than not working. I sampled a wide variety of social service programs. I unraveled food vouchers like Roman scrolls in checkout lines. I marveled at the irony of Jefferson signing the Declaration of Independence on my food stamps. I sold the ring on my finger. I stood in line for General Relief, and found myself next to a former client, recently released from a mental hospital. Who are you here for, he wanted to know. Me, I said. To borrow a phrase from Herbert Hill, I have been both a client and a constituent.

Like my father, I refused to accept my place in line. I obtained a law degree from Northeastern University Law School and worked as an attorney for a number of years. I, too, channeled my energy into political activism. I worked for META, a bilingual education law firm, and served as supervisor of Su Clínica Legal, a program for low-income Latino tenants in Chelsea, outside Boston. Now I work as a professor in the English Department at the University of Massachusetts-Amherst, teaching creative writing and Latino poetry. Given my history, I ask myself: What next? Chimney sweep? Rodeo clown?

For some poets, social class is the triangle in the orchestra, a distant tinkling. For me, the matter of social class is the beat itself, an insistent percussion (mine is a Latin jazz orchestra). In writing about social class, I pay homage, bear witness, act as advocate, and tell secrets.

I pay homage, for example, when I write about my father's struggles. "The Other Alamo" deals with his sit-in at a segregated lunch counter in San Antonio, Texas, for the privilege of being served a cheeseburger. I want to confront the complacency of those who take their privileges for granted with the news of this event. I also want to comfort those who have endured similar humiliations, hold a mirror to their faces, show them the pride there. Paying homage is about the acceptance of an inheritance, the refusal to forsake ancestors, community, class.

I bear witness when I write about my work experiences. For many years, I was a spy. Since laborers are invisible in many eyes, valued only for what their hands can do, people say and do things in front of them which reveal true motivations, hidden bigotries. My boss at the factory showroom felt free to ask me why the spics at his Air Force base always cut the lunch line because I wasn't really there for him. This invisibility has been a blessing for me. As a poet-spy, I not only saw and heard, but saw and heard differently from the people around me. As I pumped gas, no one was aware that I would write a poem about the intoxicated hearse driver who asked me for directions. As I hosed down cages coated with monkey shit, no one could predict that I would write a poem called "Do Not Put Dead Monkeys in the Freezer." The drunk I punched in the head as a bar bouncer, breaking my finger, certainly didn't anticipate I would write a poem about him. Neither did the judge in Chelsea District Court, where I argued as a lawyer, realize that I would someday write verse comparing his face to a fist.

I am an advocate when I write poems speaking on behalf of those without an opportunity to be heard, for one of the curses of segregation and subordination by class is the imposition of silence. The poems seek to release a voice caught in the collective throat. Here, I am influenced by a long Latin American tradition: Pablo Neruda, Ernesto Cardenal, Clemente Soto Vélez, Claribel Alegría. Eduardo Galeano has written, "I write for those who cannot read me." These are the human beings who, in the words of Wolfgang Binder, "run the risk of leaving this earth unrecorded." If I know Mrs. Báez, a Dominican immigrant living in the burned-out wreckage of a building torched by her landlord, then I am obligated to record her painfully dignified ritual of serving coffee to strangers. If I know Jacobo, a Guatemalan artist, a refugee from political persecution on the verge of being deported, who cleaned offices by night and painted stunning landscapes by day, I am compelled to write of his colors, his green and red. To know that a cockroach may become embedded in a child's ear is to accept responsibility for that knowledge, to communicate that knowledge for the sake of those who do not know, and those who do. How could I know what I know, and not tell what I know?

I tell secrets when I write about social class. The great secret is that class matters, very much, in this society dizzy with the illusion of classlessness. Writing about class is to write about power relationships as they really are, in their nakedness, and so to write about how this system actually works. And where better to learn about the emphasis on property over people than in court, with landlord-tenant cases? The poem, "Tires Stacked in the Hallways of Civilization," documents an actual exchange in Chelsea District Court, where a landlord admitted that there were rodents infesting the building, but justified himself by proclaiming that he allowed the tenant to have a cat. I call this my cat poem.

Secrets and silences imply censorship. I recall a rejection letter which objected that a certain poem's "political speech" was "too thinly concealed," as if the politics should not only be concealed, but *thickly* concealed. Sometimes the reaction is more crudely expressed. A seventh-grader once told me that a report he wrote about one of my books so infuriated his teacher that she confiscated not only the report, but the book as well. A prestigious literary organization was unwilling to publish an article of mine because it dealt with FBI harassment of a Puerto Rican nationalist poet, until a lawyer on their board pressured the organization to do so. This is why the breakthroughs are so gratifying. A Puerto Rican hospital administrator in Connecticut told me that he read a poem of mine, "The New Bathroom Policy at English High School," aloud at a meeting, causing the hospital to reverse its policy of forbidding patients to speak Spanish among themselves.

Too many poets maintain the myth of a society without any real class distinctions or conflict. They do so by assuming that everyone belongs to a certain elite and writing accordingly, with an elite diction full of elitist references for elite audiences. These poets reveal their class biases in unintended, and, for me, unflattering ways. Once, while judging a national poetry competition, I came across a series of vacation poems (as distinct from travel poems), written by a poet who bragged that she went to Paris and "lunched on perfect Brie." The arrogance and snobbery of that statement simply dazzled me. I was reminded of lines from Neruda, speaking of a fellow poet who ate bread every day, but had never seen a baker.

Not everyone belongs to the elite, even in the world of poetry. The damned are not only subject, but also audience, and even writers themselves. Not every poetry reading occurs on a college campus or at a bookstore. There are readings at community centers and prisons, for adult literacy, GED, and English-as-a-Second-Language programs. Not every poet works, or has always worked, as an academic. If we read the poets of the monastery, let us not forget the poets of the kitchen, who are loud and sweaty and terribly alive.

There are so many poets, in the Latino community alone, who write from the kitchen with grace and power. Jack Agüeros has given us "Sonnets from the Puerto Rican," demanding respect for his street subjects with the use of the sonnet form. Luis Rodríguez has written of "La Vida Loca," his gang days in Chicano East Los Angeles. Demetria Martinez has documented the realities of two Salvadoran refugee women in her poem "Nativity" and was prosecuted for allegedly smuggling aliens (she was acquitted, despite the fact that the poem was introduced against her as evidence). All of us write about class, not as abstraction, not with a capital C, but as a consequence of lived experience. As with any other poet, our poems are about family, friends, lovers, clients, community, self. The difference is that the people in these poems suffer from the class system in this society, rather than benefit by it.

All this is not to say that a poet who writes about these issues must necessarily forgo the concerns of language. There is no contradiction between writing about being poor, or working-class, or Latino, and writing well. When we write about the collisions of class, we are writing about conflict, and we were always told in school that conflict lies at the heart of good literature. Perhaps the vocabulary is more urgent than usual, but then again the house is on fire.

What do we want, finally, when we write from an awareness of class and its punishments? We want change, which, as Frederick Douglass pointed out, does not come without a demand. Galeano adds: "To claim that literature on its own is going to change reality would be an act of madness or arrogance. It seems to me no less foolish to deny that it can aid in making this change." This is the poem as an act of political imagination, the poet not merely as prosecutor, but as visionary. For this purpose, a poet can be as useful as a hammer. I think of all the reversals I want to see, the reversals of a poem called "Imagine the Angels of Bread": squatters evicting landlords, refugees deporting judges, immigrants crossing the border to be greeted with trumpets and drums, the food stamps of adolescent mothers auctioned like gold doubloons. I think of my father and the peace that has never been his. Here is my vision: The war is over, and Zapata's disciple is lunching on perfect Brie.

Seeing in the Dark

I want to begin with what I consider an amazing sentence, and then spend the rest of the time elaborating on what I think it means and why it's so important to writers—in particular, to poets. The sentence is from a book by an anthropologist and linguist named Leonard Bloomfield. The title of the book, published in the 1920s, is *Language*, and in this particular chapter Bloomfield is discussing the development of written language. Here's the sentence: "Language, after all, is our one way of communicating the kind of things that do not lend themselves to drawing." I would offer a couple of paraphrases: Written language is the system we have for expressing what can't be shown in a picture. And: Language is what we use to make the invisible visible.

Bloomfield's claim, and my versions of it, may at first seem surprising—even shocking—claims to make. For one thing, we're often inclined to think of language as word pictures. Also, most of us have seen some examples of the beginnings of written language—of pictographs, or little simplified pictures—a man, the sun, a tree, water, carved or painted or incised on a rock or bark—used to record an event or to send a message. Written language may have begun that way, with pictures that eventually developed into symbols, and, in some cases, into ideographs, or picture-symbols that stand for ideas. But the ultimate development of written language is the phonetic alphabet. In phonetic alphabets, like ours, the letters stand not for things or for anything visual, but for *sounds*, and it is only when we translate those marks into sounds that they take on meaning as words and sentences. When we read we use our eyes, but only long enough to hand the squiggles and marks on to the ear. As the fiction writer and philosopher William Gass says, "Just as we listen with our eyes when we read, so we see with our ears when we hear."

For the purposes of what I want to say here, there's no significant difference between spoken and written language. Written language is comparable to musical notation and has the same relationship to spoken language that musical notation has to music sung and played. Reading is indeed a kind of listening, like listening to the radio, which in turn is one way of being read to. When we listen, we see—but we see with the *mind's eye*. That's what we do—or should do—when we read, and that's what we have to do when we write. Apollinaire described it as the difference between sight and insight—what we see with our eyes open and what we see with our eyes closed.

Robert Frost said—and this was long before television had overwhelmed everyone with its literal-minded imagery—Frost said, "We value the seeing eye already. It's time we said something about the hearing ear." He also said: "The ear is the only true writer and the only true reader." I agree with that absolutely, but given the overwhelming predominance of visual imagery now, with television and computer screens, I'm worried that the ear may be going the way of the appendix and wisdom teeth and little toes—gradually disappearing because we have so little use for them.

I grew up listening to radio—at least when I wasn't reading: *The Green Hornet, Mr. Keene Tracer of Lost Persons, The Shadow, The FBI in Peace and War, Let's Pretend, Mr. Chameleon.* That last show is a good example of radio's power to stimulate the imagination: Mr. Chameleon was a detective who in each show donned a different disguise to solve the mystery. Think about that: different disguises conveyed without pictures. I suppose it's no more surprising than the fact that Edgar Bergen's ventriloquist act was also a big hit on radio. With nothing to go on but the actors' voices and a few sound effects, I pictured characters, actions, emotions, and relationships. I did the same thing when I read, listening to the voices, to what Frost refers to as "the sound of sense." So I was surprised when I first began to teach and discovered that my students had trouble with what I thought of as the automatic translation of language into imagery.

As a teaching assistant at the University of Iowa, I assigned a Dickens novel for a course on narrative exactly because I thought all its gestures were so broad and so obvious that it would be a good place to begin, and that from there we could go on to subtler stuff. But in fact, my students had enormous trouble reading the Dickens novel. The conventions and clues that stood out like so many signposts to me were invisible to them. When an old man, Twemlow, was compared at length to a table because he was so stiff, my students didn't know whether Dickens was describing a man or a table. Not long after that I assigned a different class to do a little listening: to a baseball game on the radio and to a radio drama, *CBS Radio Mystery Theater*—which painted in much broader strokes than Dickens. Though some enjoyed the shows, most said they simply hadn't been able to follow what was going on. I realized then that listening for meaning was a skill, not something people were born with, and that most students were arriving at college without it. So I spend my time teaching my students how to read—really read.

Recently I taught a graduate seminar in which we used the *Norton Anthology of Modern Poetry* and several books of modern and contemporary poetry. I had tapes of poets reading many of the assigned poems, which students listened to on their own, and as the term went on we spent more and more class time reading the poems aloud. For any poems longer than a few stanzas, we went around the table, with each student reading a stanza aloud, so there was a powerful sense of community and collaboration. It was very moving to me to hear the increasing confidence and pleasure and understanding in their readings. The week we were discussing *The Waste Land* I told my students not to reread the poem, but to *listen* to a tape of Eliot reading it. What had been a literary monument obscured by a blizzard of footnotes became for them what it was meant to be all along: a live thing in their ears, a work for the human voice. Not surprisingly, they were amazed and moved by it in a way they hadn't been before.

One more example of the pleasures of listening: there's a new translation of the *Iliad* by Robert Fagles, and a taped version of it—six tapes, nine hours long—read by Derek Jacoby. Though I had read and taught the work several times, listening has given me a sense of the structure, of some scenes and characters, and of details and pacing, that I'd never had before.

Let's go back to Bloomfield's claim: language is for expressing what *can't* be shown in a picture. But what of the old bromide that "a picture is worth a thousand words"? Here's an example of the reverse, of something that language can express that can't be shown in a picture—or in a thousand pictures. A sociologist was giving a talk to a group of Navajo. When he was finished an elderly woman came up to ask him a question. He interrupted her and said, condescendingly, "Oh, you speak English." She looked him straight in the eye and said, after a pause, "Impeccably." *Impeccably.* I can't imagine any way to draw a picture of that word.

So language isn't simply a poor substitute for what could be better shown in a picture. If that were the case a picture *would* be worth a thousand words and we wouldn't need language—indeed, it never would have developed because it would have been redundant, unnecessary. If pictures and language did the same thing, we wouldn't need language because pictures do a much better job of that kind of showing. But, as Bloomfield says, language does something else: it makes visible what is otherwise invisible, it opens a door—or doors—into what is otherwise darkness.

Think for a minute about how our bodies take in information. We have five senses: sight, hearing, taste, touch, and smell. Sight is our most prominent sense physiologically, and takes up the largest area of the sensory portion of our brains, followed by hearing, and then taste, touch, and smell, which are relatively weak in humans. Even our two strongest senses have limited capabilities: we see and hear only within certain ranges of wavelengths, we pick up only a small portion of what actually goes on in the universe, and then we create the world we know out of the fragments of information. That's the best we can do, but it's important to keep in mind how limited a view we have, and not to mistake it for everything that exists. For example, sight is our dominant sense, followed by hearing, but we know that a great deal goes on outside of the ranges that are visible and audible *to us*, what we can pick up. Beyond that, according to physicists and astronomers most of what exists—over 90 percent of what exists in the universe—is *invisible*. On the one hand, this fact makes the visible world—the world that's visible to us—extremely valuable because it's so rare. At the same time, the immensity of the invisible should tell us how crucial it is that we have tools for exploring the invisible. This brings us once again to Bloomfield's assertion that language is for expressing what can't be shown in a picture.

I think language began in the dark, not the light. The primary purpose of language isn't to communicate basic information like, "Enemies are coming," or, "There are fresh bananas just over the hill," or, "I want you." For those things we could get by with gestures and a few grunts and hoots. Rousseau thought that musical sounds accompanied or preceded speech, and said of its origins: ". . . it is not hunger or thirst, but love, hatred, pity, and anger which drew from humans their first utterances." Vico and Heidegger, among others, hypothesized that the metaphorical use of language preceded the literal and scientific. William Gass makes the same point repeatedly in his essays, arguing that it was the musical, metaphorical, playful impulses that drove the development of language and have been its primary shapers.

Think again about that word *impeccable*, and what fine-tuning of perception it implies: *irreproachable, faultless, without sin*. Or think about synonyms. It's probably true that no two words have identical meanings. Here's one example from a thesaurus of how a group of words that mean almost the same thing subdivide that one meaning into a number of fine distinctions or shadings, as if the color blue were being divided into dozens of tints all the way from aquamarine to navy. Here are just a few of the terms the thesaurus lists under *happiness: gladness, delight, delectation, joy, cheerfulness, exhilaration, exuberance, high spirits, glee, sunshine, gaiety, rapture, elation, exaltation, ecstasy, bliss*. Each of these words makes visible—at least to the mind's eye—a slightly different shade of meaning.

Language is a tool for seeing in the dark, for seeing with our eyes closed. Those who can't use it are blind to everything except the crudest categories of the visible world, and can't make much sense even of those because they can't put their thoughts and emotions into words.

Now what does this understanding of language have to do with reading and writing poems? Obviously it means that to understand any poem you have to *hear* it, hear the words, the rhythms—and most of all, the voice that's saying the poem. Sometimes that takes many readings or listenings before it all comes clear. What you're listening for is what Frost referred to as "the sound of sense." He said, "I have consciously set myself to make music out of what I may call the sound of sense. . . . The best place to get the sound of sense is from voices behind a door that cuts off the words. . . . It is pure sound, pure form." Elsewhere he says: "A sentence is a sound in itself on which other sounds called words may be strung." Notice that Frost said he was "making music." For all their differences, I think Frost and Pound had a lot in common. Pound, of course, spoke about composing with the cadence of the musical phrase, and though he and Frost employed very different strategies for making poems musical, both assumed that language itself is musical.

What I'm talking about here is *prosody*—not simply in terms of the narrower definition that applies to the formal elements of poetry, but the prosody of language as a whole, all the elements smaller and larger than words that convey meaning: assonance, consonance, alliteration, rhyme, stress—but especially larger units such as phrasing, pitch, intonation, and so on—the elements that, as Frost said, you can hear through a closed door. You could certainly tell, for example, if two people were fighting, if someone asked a question, if one person were pleading and the other refusing, and so on.

In written language, punctuation and context carry a lot of this information. William Gass says, in an essay titled "Habitations of the Word": "The writer must make up for the loss of the spoken context. . . . Above all, the written word must be set down so that it rises up immediately in its readers to the level of the ear . . . it asks, that is, to be performed . . . it asks to be said, to be sung." In another essay, "The Soul inside the Sentence," Gass gives examples of some literary sentences he admires and says of them: "These sentences have a psychology because they have a soul; and how anything like a soul . . . can contrive to squeeze itself among so many syllables . . . how any series of ordinary words . . . can rise up from the page, not merely like a snake from its basket, but into immaterial lengths of song, as though the serpent had become the music which entranced it . . . that is a rare bit of magic. . . ." In that same essay he goes on to say:

[As infants we are] surrounded by our own scent; slowly aware of our limbs, we soon swaddle ourselves in our own sounds, as we shall live later with the dearest companion of our life: the voice of consciousness, the words which become the self. We should never forget then, that from the very beginning, when the word made the world, the word has been one of the most important "objects" in human experience. We were born into language as into perception, pain, and pleasure . . . we manufactured our own noise, and long before we knew the meanings words bore, we knew the meanings which bore them, the emotional contexts . . . in which they were formed.

It is a truism to say that music is closely and powerfully linked to our emotions, and that's just as true for the music of language. In his book *Music and the Mind*, Anthony Storr suggests that infants register those elements of language first. He says: "Early mother-infant exchanges use components of language more concerned with emotional expressiveness than with factual information." In Frost's terms, we learn the *sounds* of sense before we learn the specifics. We learn the music before we learn the words.

When we read a poem we should listen as if it were a piece of music—and it is, if it's any good. That's also why the best answer to "What does this poem mean?" is "Read it again." I once heard James Tate say, of people who complain about the difficulty of John Ashbery's poems, "Why don't they just listen? All they have to do is listen." It may not be all we have to do, but it's certainly the place to begin, and to return to. All the other work we do—looking words up in a dictionary, looking up allusions, studying the rhythm, the lines, the line breaks, learning what we can about historical context—is all in the service of *hearing* the poem as precisely as possible.

What we're listening for, most of all, is the voice that's speaking the poem. In poems, the primary device that carries and controls and shapes the music—the sound of sense—is the voice that speaks the poem. It is the voice of the poem that makes the invisible visible.

Sometimes that speaking voice belongs to a particular person, a character we learn something about in the course of reading the poem. The most obvious examples are monologues, dialogues, and persona poems, where a speaker or speakers are identified. Frost wrote many such poems, and his second book, *North of Boston*, consisted entirely of such pieces. He was a genius at creating the illusion of natural dialogue in a metrical poem. Here are a couple of examples from his poem "The Witch of Coos." The speaker stops overnight at a farm where he's told a story by the mother and son living there. It's about bones, a skeleton that used to be buried in the cellar but escaped long ago to the attic, where it's been nailed inside ever since. The son says:

It left the cellar forty years ago
And carried itself like a pile of dishes
Up one flight from the cellar to the kitchen,
Another from the kitchen to the bedroom,
Right past both father and mother, and neither stopped it.
I was the baby: I don't know where I was.

And a little further along the mother describes the escape of the bones from the cellar:

My first impulse was to get to the knob
And hold the door. But the bones didn't try
The door; they halted helpless on the landing,
Waiting for things to happen in their favor.
The faintest rustling ran all through them.
I never could have done the thing I did
If the wish hadn't been too strong in me
To see how they were mounted for this walk.
I had a vision of them put together
Not like a man but like a chandelier.
So suddenly I flung the door wide on him.
A moment he stood balancing with emotion,
And all but lost himself. (A tongue of fire
Flashed out and licked along his upper teeth.
Smoke rolled inside the sockets of his eyes.)
Then he came at me with one hand outstretched,
The way he did in life once; but this time
I struck the hand off brittle on the floor,
And fell back from him on the floor myself.
The finger-pieces slid in all directions.
(Where did I see one of those pieces lately?
Hand me my button box—it must be there.)

But of course those are the voices of characters *in* the poem, not the voice of the poem itself. Two of Frost's best known poems provide clear examples of the distinction. Recently someone told me he liked Frost's poems because he agreed with Frost that "Good fences make good neighbors." But it's the *neighbor*, not the speaker of the poem, who makes that

claim. The speaker wonders if he could get the neighbor, whom he compares to an "old-stone savage armed," to question his belief, to understand, "Something there is that doesn't love a wall." But the neighbor
simply repeats his certainty that "Good fences make good neighbors."
And in "The Road Not Taken," the speaker is *not* arguing that he "took
the road less traveled by, / And that made all the difference." He has said,
explicitly, that the two diverging roads were "worn really about the
same," that the two were in fact equally traveled, but that after the fact—
"Somewhere ages and ages hence"—he will explain his choice, to himself and others, by claiming that one road had been less traveled.

A first-person speaker can appear in a number of guises. The voice of a
poem might be that of a first-person speaker in action:

> I went to turn the grass once after one
> Who mowed it in the dew before the sun . . .
>   —"A Tuft of Flowers"

or that of a first-person speaker thinking aloud:

> My sorrow, when she's here with me
>   Thinks these dark days of autumn rain
> Are beautiful as days can be;
> She loves the bare, the withered tree;
>   She walks the sodden pasture lane . . .
>   —"My November Guest"

or a first-person plural, speaking for two:

> They leave us so to the way we took,
>   As two in whom they were proved mistaken . . .
>   —"Two Look at Two"

or a first-person plural speaking for many:

> We make ourselves a place apart
>   Behind light words that tease and flout,

> But oh, the agitated heart
> Till someone really find us out. . . .
>
> —"Revelation"

The poem's speaking voice doesn't have to be any form of first person, of course. It might be the voice of a third-person narrator:

> These pools that, though in forests, still reflect
> The total sky almost without defect,
> And like the flowers beside them, chill and shiver,
> Will like the flowers beside them soon be gone,
> And yet not out by any brook or river,
> But up by roots to bring dark foliage on. . . .
>
> —"Spring Pools"

This third-person narrative voice is one that's familiar to us from childhood, from fairy tales. Here's the opening of "Snow White":

Once upon a time in the middle of winter, when the flakes of snow were falling like feathers from the sky, a Queen sat at a window sewing, and the frame of the window was made of black ebony. And while she was sewing and looking out of the window at the snow, she pricked her finger with the needle and three drops of blood fell upon the snow. And the red looked pretty upon the white snow, and she thought to herself: "Would that I had a child as white as snow, as red as blood, and as black as the wood of the window frame."

Here are the opening lines of three different poems by the Polish poet Wislawa Szymborska. You can hear how immediately they establish the poem's speaking voice: "No one in my family has ever died of love . . ." ("Family Album"); "So that is his mother . . ." ("Born of Woman"); "We drew lots, who would go and see him . . ." ("Report from the Hospital").

But sometimes we can't be sure at the beginning of a poem just what the narrative voice is. For example, Elizabeth Bishop's poem "At the Fishhouses" seems to begin with the voice of a third-person narrator:

> Although it is a cold evening,
> down by one of the fishhouses
> an old man sits netting,

> his net, in the gloaming almost invisible
> a dark purple-brown,
> and his shuttle worn and polished.
> The air smells so strong of codfish
> it makes one's nose run and one's eyes water.
> The five fishhouses have steeply peaked roofs
> and narrow cleated gangplanks slant up
> to storerooms in the gables
> for the wheelbarrows to be pushed up and down on.
> All is silver: the heavy surface of the sea,
> swelling slowly as if considering spilling over,
> is opaque, but the silver of the benches,
> the lobster pots, and masts, scattered
> among the wild jagged rocks,
> is of an apparent translucence
> like the small old buildings with an emerald moss
> growing on their shoreward walls.
> The big fish tubs are completely lined
> with layers of beautiful herring scales . . .

But then there's a surprise:

> The old man accepts a Lucky Strike.
> He was a friend of my grandfather . . .

and we realize that the poem has been spoken all along by an unobtrusive first-person speaker. Other Bishop poems feature a similar narrator. Here's the opening of one called "Insomnia":

> The moon in the bureau mirror
> looks out a million miles
> (and perhaps with pride, at herself,
> but she never, never smiles). . . .

The speaker doesn't appear in this one until the last line—in fact, the last word—and then it's in a reflection, where the real world is reversed:

> where left is always right,
> where the shadows are really the body,

>where we stay awake all night,
>where the heavens are shallow as the sea
>is now deep, and you love me.

Although it's a risky strategy to use, the voice of the poem may be something other than human. In Louise Glück's Pulitzer Prize–winning book *The Wild Iris*, many of the poems are spoken by flowers. "The Red Poppy" begins:

>The great thing
>is not having
>a mind. Feelings:
>oh, I have those. . . .

And ends:

>. . . I am speaking now
>the way you do. I speak
>because I am shattered.

Sometimes the poem addresses the reader directly, as in these opening lines from Ashbery's "Paradoxes and Oxymorons":

>The poem is concerned with language on a very plain level.
>Look at it talking to you. You look out a window
>Or pretend to fidget. You have it but you don't have it.
>You miss it, it misses you. You miss each other.

Voice in a poem can be as recognizable as a singer's voice on a record. Here's Emily Dickinson:

>There's a certain Slant of light
>Winter afternoons—
>That oppresses, like the Heft
>of cathedral Tunes—

or:

>"Hope" is the thing with feathers—
>That perches in the soul—

> And sings the tune without the words—
> And never stops—at all—

In Charles Simic's poems, a distinctive voice is usually audible from the first words spoken. Here are a few opening lines from prose poems in his Pulitzer Prize–winning collection *The World Doesn't End*: "My mother was a braid of black smoke"; "We were so poor I had to take the place of the cheese in the mousetrap"; "My guardian angel was afraid of the dark." And here's the first stanza of his poem "The Partial Explanation," which seems to whisper in your ear from its opening line:

> Seems like a long time
> Since the waiter took my order.
> Grimy little luncheonette,
> The snow falling outside. . . .

What does all this have to do with *writing* poems? There, too, the major part of our work is listening. But in this case we're listening for the voice of our own poems. Not that it will always be the same voice, of course— there will be different ones. But as we work we're doing something like tuning across a radio dial, listening through all the squeals and static for that voice, however faint, that we recognize as the right one. We're groping our way in the dark, and we have nothing but language and the music of language to guide us.

Here are brief examples from a well-known poet before and after he found his poetic voice. The first is a stanza from an early poem called "Desires of Men and Women":

> Exasperated, won, you conjure a mansion,
> The absolute butlers in the spacious hall,
> Old silver, lace, and privacy, a house
> Where nothing has for years been out of place,
> Neither shoe-horn nor affection been out of place,
> Breakfast in summer on the eastern terrace,
> All just and all grace.

You can hear the poem's intelligence and technical skill, but whatever voice it has is too thin, too anonymous and distanced, too far from any felt speaking voice to bring the poem to life. As Storr says in *Music and the Mind*, "Music is rooted in the body." So, of course, must the voice of the poem be. Here's the opening of one of that same poet's later poems, after he had found his distinctive voice and grounded it in the body's music:

> There sat down, once, a thing on Henry's heart
> so heavy, if he had a hundred years
> & more, & weeping, sleepless, in all them time
> Henry could not make good.
> Starts again always in Henry's ears
> the little cough somewhere, an odour, a chime.
>> —Berryman, "Dream Song #29"

I think this posture of listening is extremely helpful when we're revising, too. Sometimes we're tempted to try to insist on our first idea for a poem, what *we* intended to say. But the poem always knows more than we do, if we just listen and follow where it takes us.

With all this emphasis on voice, what role does imagery play? In the best poems, the imagery follows from the voice, is created and conveyed by the poem's language and voice. The voice of the poem creates the vision we see—whether the images are realistic or surrealistic, of this world or other-worldly.

I've come back to a very traditional notion of the poem as lyric, as words and music fused to express—not the self, which is mostly boring and trivial—but to express complex thoughts and feelings, to *create* a play of light and shadow where before there was nothing, to light a match in the dark, to whisper in the ear, to nudge open a door in the mind.

Imagine what it was like for our ancestors, creatures who could walk upright and use their hands and make tools, who were just developing the first glimmerings of self-consciousness, just becoming aware of themselves, of their differences from other animals, and of the passage of time—just becoming the only animals who could foresee their own deaths. There they were, no light but the moon and stars and occasional fire, frightened of the dark. Out of that fear and into that darkness, they—we—began to sing.

ELLEN BRYANT VOIGT

A *Moment's Thought*

[ROPEWALK WRITERS' RETREAT]

> . . . a line will take us hours maybe;
> Yet if it does not seem a moment's thought,
> Our stitching and unstitching has been naught.
> —Yeats, "Adam's Curse"

In *Dr. Zhivago* (the movie), there is a scene in which handsome, mustached Omar Sharif, surrogate for Pasternak, bundled up against the dangerous cold in his empty dacha, with Julie Christie and Geraldine Chaplin relegated off-screen, is composing a love poem. While the theme song strums softly in the background, the camera pans the vast snow-blown, wolf-haunted steppes, moving in slowly to show the poet sitting alone in a large room at a low table, alternately staring out the window and bending down to his heavy-weight bond paper. He pauses; chews his pen; adjusts his ragged gloves and long scarf; then balls the paper into a wad and throws it to the floor. Music swells. The candle flickers (surely there was a candle). He starts again, muttering under his visible breath; scratches a line; sighs; again wads and chucks it. Camera cuts to the wolves (passing of time), within yards of the house by now, returns to the brow-furrowed poet, his feet in drifts of discarded drafts as if in snow. Finally, Omar gazes upward, music grows louder, the mustache curves into a smile, the orthodontically ideal teeth sparkle. Close-up of his hand: the pen is moving suddenly fluently over the page, supplying the rhymed and metered lines of the completed poem.

Don't blame Hollywood: it is a received image of long standing, as is this perennial from the Q and A after a reading: "Where do you get your ideas?" What's unimaginable is *doing the thing at all*. The public believes that a novel requires only a few months off from work and a used Underwood, but poems lurk in the shallows, occluded but whole, needing like fish the right bait and a little luck. Except we don't call it luck: we call it "inspiration," and whether they've seen the movie or not, this image of themselves is where most young poets begin—without the wolves, without the violins, and also too often without the debris of false starts and botched drafts.

Not that it *never* happens that way; poets, like athletes, sometimes find "the zone" where every shot swishes through the basket (though seldom in rhymed pentameter)—usually during a period of fluency in a new, newly comfortable mode. But it is a tyrannical model. Notice, in the more sophisticated original, articulated in 1800 by William Wordsworth in his Preface to the *Lyrical Ballads*, the aggressive modifier:

For *all* good poetry is the spontaneous overflow of powerful feelings. [my italics]

Of course, as with blurbs that retain the desirable adjective and suppress the otherwise negative review, Wordsworth's full sentence is often left unquoted:

For all good poetry is the spontaneous overflow of powerful feelings; and though this be true, Poems to which any value can be attached were never produced on any variety of subjects but by a man who, being possessed of more than usual organic sensibility, had also thought long and deeply.

There they are, the Scylla and Charybdis of the art: the special gift and the elusiveness of its fruition; "more than usual organic sensibility" and long deep thought; or, in the American adaptation, eyes to the ceiling, wads of white paper on the floor.

Even in cliché, as in the original, the formulation nods to paradox: that a poem derives from both receptivity and active will, that it requires both imagination and technique. Two muses, then—or Nietzsche's two gods of art, an id and a superego: Dionysius, god of wine and orgy, of feeling and flow and spontaneity; and Apollo, stern god of light, order, balance, the cognitive mind. The danger, and not just for beginning poets, is that in profile they seem all too much like handsome, exuberant youth on the one hand, and cautious, pedestrian middle age on the other. And that's been enough to give revision a bad reputation, odor of the clerk, the drudge, and the nerd.

The bias was there from the start, in Wordsworth's call for an organic poetry, one disassociated from philosophy and realigned with the mystics.

I have said that poetry is the spontaneous overflow of powerful feelings: it takes its origin from emotion recollected in tranquility; the emotion is contemplated till, by a species of reaction, the tranquility gradually disappears, and an emotion, kindred to that which was before the subject of contemplation is gradually produced, and does itself actually exist in the mind. In this mood successful composition generally begins, and in a mood similar to this it is carried on. . . .

Elsewhere in his preface Wordsworth defines "this mood" as a "state of excitement," about which he adds, "ideas and feelings do not, in that state, succeed each other in accustomed order"—allowing Apollo at least into the theatre. But the stage directions for Omar Sharif are clear: emotion is both wellspring and bucket, lens and subject: the poet is to be transported.

Meanwhile, there has appeared, since Wordsworth, another formulation, redistributing the weight: Einstein's definition of genius as 10 percent inspiration, 90 percent perspiration or Flannery O'Connor's wonderful crack that she wasn't a genius, merely talented, so had to work very hard at her fiction. A shift away from the primacy of the natural and the received underlies Eliot's regard for the Metaphysical Poets' passionate *thought*, the New Critical attention to irony, paradox, figure, and wit, and Yeats's cautionary:

> Better go down upon your marrow-bones
> And scrub a kitchen pavement, or break stones
> Like an old pauper, in all kinds of weather;
> For to articulate sweet sounds together
> Is to work harder than all these. . . .
>
> —"Adam's Curse"

This is, of course, still the Orphic ideal, poet as special case, a "more than usual organic sensibility" (although their adjective might have been "erudite" rather than "organic") but the High Modernists focused on the gap between that sensibility and the page. Pound's definition of image, his insistence on poetry "at least as good as good prose," his skill as an editor and his "Ezuversity," restored both educated intelligence and a work ethic to the notion of what a poet actually does. For a model we might take Hemingway, doggedly writing his requisite number of paragraphs every day, or Dylan Thomas when sober, hours taking out a comma, hours putting it back.

In Yeats's case, many of his poems are first signaled in manuscript by a prose note sketching a subject, often followed by the end words of a rhyme scheme. (These materials are available from several sources. I recommend Curtis Bradford's *Yeats at Work*.) For instance, this notebook entry:

> Topic for poem. School children and the thought that life will waste them, perhaps that no possible life can fulfill their own dreams or even their teacher's hope. Bring in the old thought that life prepares for what never happens.

Seeing tranquility lowered here to hypothermia, one would hardly think to ask Yeats, "Where did you get that idea?"—the kind of query he tended to deflect with high-class voodoo (a sudden smell of roses, voices dictating to his enrapt wife)—but rather, "What happened?" between the first logged source and the masterpiece, "Among School Children." That question is answered only obliquely, in the poem's serene—one might say inspired—closure:

> O body swayed to music, O brightening glance,
> How can we know the dancer from the dance?

The important distinction between the two formulations, then, may not lie in the popular but simplistic opposition of inspiration versus labor. Seamus Heaney, in *Preoccupations*, shrewdly maps the common ground:

> I chose the word "makings" for the title ["The Makings of a Music"] because it gestures towards the testings and hesitations of the workshop, the approaches towards utterance, the discovery of lines and then the intuitive extension of the vital element in those lines over a whole passage. . . . The given line (*donné*), the phrase or

cadence which haunts the ear and the eager parts of the mind, this is the tuning fork to which the whole music of the poem is orchestrated, *that out of which* the overall melodies are worked for or calculated. It is my impression that this haunting or *donné occurs to all poets in much the same way, arbitrarily,* with a sense of promise, as an alertness, a hankering, a readiness. It is also my impression that the quality of the music in the finished poem has to do with *the way the poet proceeds to respond to his donné.* If he surrenders to it, allows himself to be carried by its initial rhythmic suggestiveness, to become somnambulist after its invitations, then we will have a music not unlike Wordsworth's, hypnotic, swimming with the current of its form rather than against it. If, on the other hand, instead of surrendering to the drift of the *original, generating* rhythm, the poet seeks to discipline it, to harness its energies in order to drive other parts of his mind into motion, then we will have a music not unlike Yeats's, affirmative, seeking to master rather than to mesmerize the ear, swimming strongly against the current of its form. [my italics]

This is beautifully written and convincing, allowing for the differences in temperament between Wordsworth's "mood" of composition and Yeats's pauper breaking stones, but maintaining the primacy of a crucial generative moment. In Heaney's analysis—as, I suspect, in the self-edited memories of making our own poems—both examples, Wordsworth and Yeats, presume an *initial* donné: both require that which is visited on us "arbitrarily," or emerges from the subconscious, and then will be either followed or struggled against as the poet "proceeds to respond to his donné" (Heaney) in "a species of reaction" (Wordsworth). Dionysius, then Apollo; the right side of the brain, then the left; presentiment, then articulation; music, then language; Valéry's "vers donné," what is given, then "vers calculé," what is made.

What I'd adjust in this narrative is the fixed sequence, extending Heaney's point about relatively active or passive engagement with the muse. The acts of focused attention ("alertness") which poems require need not always "occur[ ] to all poets in much the same way, arbitrarily," but may evolve from the "habit of art" (O'Connor quoting Maritain) or a "rage for order" (Wallace Stevens); instructive cadence can follow, rather than always precede, rational application of craft; and if visitation cannot be willed it remains, nonetheless, a disguised part of the will, and may be willfully invited. Following the prose notes as they do, Yeats's auditions for stanza form and rhyme scheme strike me as just such an invitation, stone struck against stone until one finally sparks and a resonant organization of the material begins in that light. From there, under the litter of subsequent drafts, one can see the essential poem emerge, see the fusion of thought and feeling, music and idea—what Graham Hough calls "luminosity"—not precipitate but actually *arise* from prosaic calculation. Even Wordsworth allowed as much, restricting his crucial "species of reaction," in whose thrall the pen races across the page, to "a man who . . . had thought long and deeply." In the compositional mood, or state of excitement, he said, "ideas and feelings do not . . . succeed each other in accustomed order." There lies great encouragement: vision may be the fruit of technique, not only its precursor, and the donné need not be *first* cause. Think of Pope's "happy coincidence in search of a rhyme"—the sheer generative power of a restrictive form. Or Keats setting out on yet another disposable sonnet, such as he and friends often penned for amusement in Leigh Hunt's parlor, and writing "On First Looking into Chapman's Homer."

Nevertheless—no matter the proportions, no matter the sequence—the problem with the dialectic model remains: What finally accounts for the firing across the synapse, bridging, in communicable text, craft and cadence, will and vision, labored-for precision and elusive grace? Well, there is this from Lewis Thomas, physician, research scientist, and wonderful essayist:

> A solitary ant, afield, cannot be considered to have much of anything on his mind; indeed, with only a few neurons strung together by fibers, he can't be imagined to have a mind at all, much less a thought. He is more like a ganglion on legs. Four ants together, or ten, encircling a dead moth on a path, begin to look more like an idea. They fumble and shove, gradually moving the food toward the Hill, but as though by blind chance. It is only when you watch the dense mass of thousands of ants, crowded together around the Hill, blackening the ground, that you begin to see the whole beast, and now you observe it thinking, planning, calculating. It is an intelligence . . . with crawling bits for its wits.
>
> —*The Lives of a Cell*

"Crawling bits"—Thomas anticipated almost entirely the latest surmises about the human brain. The recent bicameral (and thoroughly Nietzschean) model—right brain for intuition, emotion, art, and music; left brain for logic, rational thought, and language—is already outdated;

such neat divisions were never verified except in pathology. In its place has come the concept of "modularity": that a lifetime of data is not stored on labeled shelves in the closet but processed multiply, by distinct networks of differing function, this very sentence dismantled into its component parts, one set of ganglions taking care of the nouns, another the verbs, another flashing up your own shelf, in your own closet at home, from the image depot, a separate hard-wired board parsing out the syntax you may have been born to, the brain's musicians tuning up to the lexical and syntactical repetitions I'm using, and a brand-new neural pathway extending itself like algae shot with Rapid-Gro to accommodate this new word, "modularity," and its baggage, "modules" and "modern" and "insularity" and "modular housing" and even, from the rhyming crew, "nodules," even "noodles." *Thought*, it seems, is not the linear storage and retrieval system we know from computers. And if Thomas's analogy holds for the way we receive, process, and act on information, consider what must be happening when we set out to produce a poem, a complex construct made from intuition, observation, experience, erudition, music, memory, and feeling—what Coleridge called "the blossom and the fragrancy of all human knowledge, human thoughts, human passions, motions, language."

Thomas suggests a model for that as well:

"Stigmergy" is a new word, invented recently by Grasse to explain the nest-building behavior of termites, perhaps generalizable to other complex activities of social animals. The word is made of Greek roots meaning "to incite to work," and Grasse's intention was to indicate that it is *the product of work itself that provides both the stimulus and instructions for further work* [my italics].

He arrived at this after long observation of the construction of termite nests, which excepting perhaps a man-made city are the most formidable edifices in nature. The interiors of the nests are like a three-dimensional maze, intricate arrangements of spiraling galleries, corridors, and arched vaults, ventilated and air-conditioned. There are great caverns for the gardens of fungi on which the termites depend for their nourishment, perhaps also as a source of heat. There is a rounded vaulted chamber for the queen, called the royal cell. The fundamental structural unit, on which the whole design is based, is the arch. . . .

Termites are . . . extraordinary in the way they seem to accumulate intelligence as they gather together. Grasse placed a handful of termites in a dish filled with soil and fecal pellets and watched what they did. . . . they all simply ran around, picking up pellets at random and dropping them again. Then, by chance, two or three pellets happened to light on top of each other, and this transformed the behavior of everyone. Now they displayed the greatest interest and directed their attention obsessively to the primitive column, adding new pellets and fragments of earth. After reaching a certain height, the construction stopped *unless* another column was being formed nearby; in this case, the structure changed from a column to an arch, bending off in a smooth curve . . . [and] the arch was joined.

It is not known how the chains of termites building one column know when to turn toward the crew on the adjacent column, or how, when the time comes, they manage the flawless joining of the arches. [When] the stimuli set them off, building collectively instead of shifting things about . . . they react as if alarmed. They become agitated, excited, and then they begin working, like artists.

"The product of work itself . . . provides both the stimulus and instructions for further work." Our mistake, perhaps, has been to privilege one module over the other in our narratives of the creative process. To mythologize—externalize—discovery is to infantilize the poet; to overcultivate the will, on the other hand, is to perpetuate the conventional in form and thought, endless replicas of "Endymion" and never Keats's odes.

Consider a first extant draft (backs of envelopes, penciled napkins, or a dreamed image not having been preserved) from Elizabeth Bishop's manuscript papers, entitled, alternately, "How To Lose Things?" "The Gift Of Losing Things?" and "The Art Of Losing Things." (See figure 1.) The draft suggests a modular mind at work: a dead moth on the path (mislaid car keys or glasses) and a solitary ant, then four ants, ten, circling it, fumbling and shoving. The bossy logical ants are busy with plans—

> One might begin . . .

> The thing to do is to begin . . .

> Mostly, one begins . . .

the tactical ants are trying out pronouns—

> One begins, one is making progress . . .

> I really want to introduce myself . . .

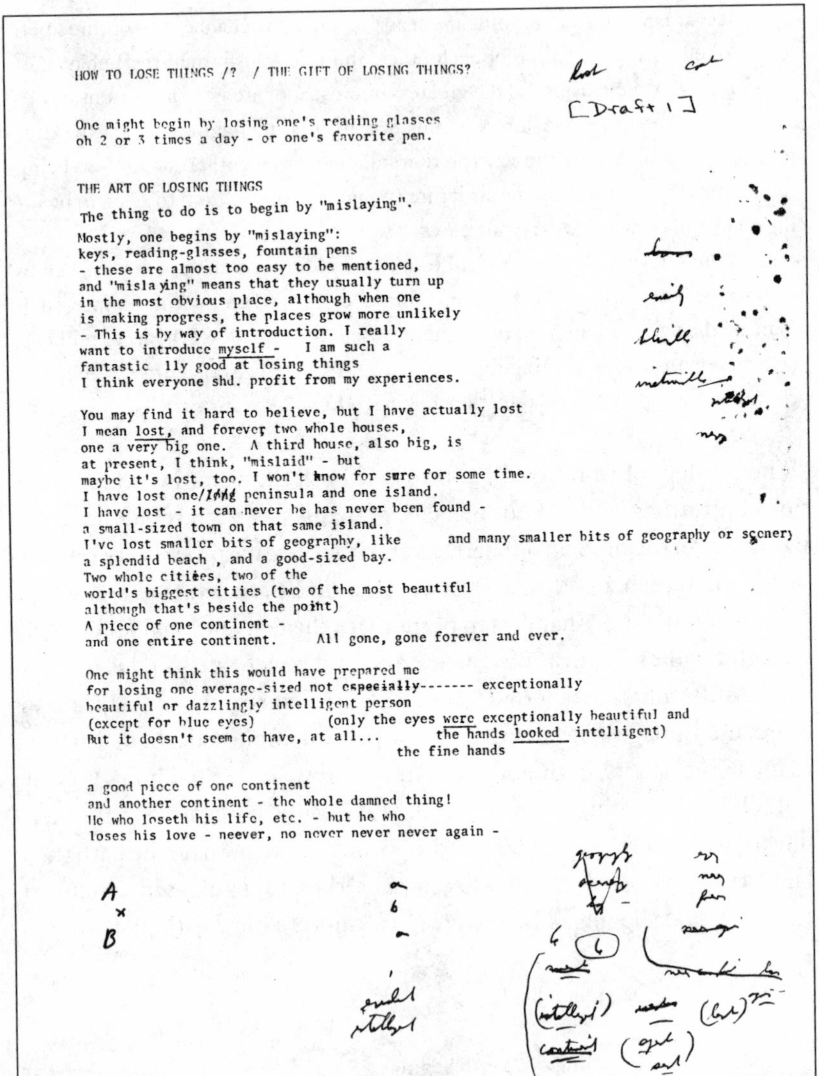

HOW TO LOSE THINGS /? / THE GIFT OF LOSING THINGS?   *lost*   *col*

[Draft 1]

One might begin by losing one's reading glasses
oh 2 or 3 times a day - or one's favorite pen.

THE ART OF LOSING THINGS

The thing to do is to begin by "mislaying".

Mostly, one begins by "mislaying":
keys, reading-glasses, fountain pens
- these are almost too easy to be mentioned,
and "mislaying" means that they usually turn up
in the most obvious place, although when one
is making progress, the places grow more unlikely
- This is by way of introduction. I really
want to introduce myself -   I am such a
fantastic lly good at losing things
I think everyone shd. profit from my experiences.

You may find it hard to believe, but I have actually lost
I mean lost, and forever two whole houses,
one a very big one.   A third house, also big, is
at present, I think, "mislaid" - but
maybe it's lost, too. I won't know for sure for some time.
I have lost one/that peninsula and one island.
I have lost - it can never be has never been found -
a small-sized town on that same island.
I've lost smaller bits of geography, like   and many smaller bits of geography or scenery
a splendid beach , and a good-sized bay.
Two whole cities, two of the
world's biggest citiies (two of the most beautiful
although that's beside the point)
A piece of one continent -
and one entire continent.   All gone, gone forever and ever.

One might think this would have prepared me
for losing one average-sized not especially------- exceptionally
beautiful or dazzlingly intelligent person
(except for blue eyes)   (only the eyes were exceptionally beautiful and
But it doesn't seem to have, at all...   the hands looked intelligent)
                                                   the fine hands

a good piece of one continent
and another continent - the whole damned thing!
He who loseth his life, etc. - but he who
loses his love - neever, no never never never again -

A
 x
B

figure 1

You may find it hard to believe . . .

One might think this would have prepared me . . .

He who loseth his life, etc. . . .

the ethical ants object from the sidelines—

these are almost too easy to be mentioned . . .

I have actually lost I mean *lost*, and forever . . .

maybe it's lost too. I won't know for sure for some time . . .

the adolescent ants are talking back and acting out ("only the eyes *were* exceptionally beautiful . . ."), the literate ants cite the Bible, the sentimental ants break down and weep ("All gone, gone forever and ever"), the musical ants break into song ("and MAny SMALLer BITS of ge- OGraphy)—

Or maybe that's the wrong insect. Is there, in fact, a dead moth fortuitously on the path? Or is the absent-mindedness what Richard Hugo called the false, the triggering, subject, and the poet in her long habit of composition was "picking up pellets at random and dropping them again" until "by chance, two or three pellets happened to light on top of each other." After the first long verse paragraph, we can chart something accruing: a verb suddenly predominates, "lost / —I mean *lost*," occurring in lines 1, 2, 5, 6, 7, 9; and there is other close repetition—houses/house, island/island, small-sized/smaller, two whole cities/two of the world's biggest cities/(two of the most beautiful . . .), a piece of one continent/one entire continent. As if "[t]he product of work itself . . . provide[d] both the stimulus and instructions for further work."

. . . this transformed the behavior of everyone. Now they displayed the greatest interest and directed their attention obsessively to the primitive column, adding new pellets and fragments of earth. After reaching a certain height, the construction stopped *unless* another column was being formed nearby. . . .

After a short stanza of assertion and contradiction, after picking up again the dropped stitch ("a good piece of one continent / and another continent"), after an outburst of frustration ("the whole damned thing!") and a dead-end reference ("He who loseth his life, etc."), after an outburst of uncontainable grief and citation from Lear ("neever, no never never never again-"), the top-heavy "primitive column" now teetering on its frail footing of keys, glasses, and pens—construction stops. But another column is forming in the margin—

A	a
X	b
B	a

the refrain and rhyme patterns for a villanelle, plus a number (6 words needed for X) and some end-word candidates: ever/never/forever; geography/scenery/-ly/easily/instinctively; intelligent/continent/spent/sent/lent/evident.

So far, nothing here necessarily contradicts either Wordsworth or Heaney—the page is full of hesitancies, approaches, the marginalia are primarily musical (one line of iambic pentameter, clearly added later, sets the cadence, and the traditional form will organize it)—although, if the biographers are right and the blue eyes are Alice Methfessel's, the grief breaking through the poet's "tranquility" is less recollected (Lota de Soares's suicide) than anticipated. But neither Wordsworth nor Heaney nor Bishop's biographers quite translate for the general reader the extent to which the working poet sees, in initial drafts, a formal challenge. The essential problems presented by the draft center around tone—which now yaws from flip to anguished, from sarcastic to maudlin—and the high degree of repetition, born of obsession and itself generative but spinning the poem out of control. Bishop's response: the discipline of an existing traditional form which converts reiteration into refrain. Whereby "the structure changed from a column to an arch, bending off in a smooth curve . . . [and] the arch was joined." By the next draft Bishop is committed to the villanelle with a secure opening (and recurrent) line: "The art of losing isn't hard to master." Now the work will have purpose and focus, building the nest's interior, the "three-dimensional maze, intricate arrangements of spiraling galleries, corridors . . . arched vaults . . . great caverns for the gardens of fungi . . . a rounded vaulted chamber for the queen, called the royal cell."

But doing so will take at least six months and fifteen more drafts. In them Bishop seems to be laboring not merely "to articulate sweet sounds together," transliterating epiphany, but to achieve a moment of vision, of insight, that would accommodate Coleridge's "reconciliation of opposites"—the tight-lipped self-dismissive tone embodied in that opening line and the casual quotidian detail, on the one hand, and on the other the unspeakable fear and self-reproach that bar acknowledgment of genuine loss and sank the earliest efforts at the poem. Bishop does not seek entry at the point closest to the emotion; rather, Brett Millier reports, the next two drafts "work mostly on the first four stanzas, whittling the catalog of losses into a discreet and resonant form and setting the rhyme scheme firmly." In the fifth and sixth drafts, Bishop's focus centers on the final stanza, again breaking under the weight of the tonal shift:

> The art of losing's not so hard to master
> But won't help in *think of that disaster*
> No—I am lying—
>
> (draft 5)

> The art of losing's not so hard to master
> until that point & then it
> fails & is disaster—
>
> (draft 6)

Draft 7 stops short of the final stanza, and the eighth seems to undo previous work, severely, with new opening tercet (compressing the earlier nine lines into three) and end-word schemata, and a start at closure with most of the lines crossed out.

Millier assumes "some time passed between the eighth and ninth drafts, for all the later attempts are typed and contain completed versions of all six stanzas." Unresolved in the interim was the poem's epiphany and resolution, that bridge from the least trivial ("continent") to the most significant (the beloved), from supportable to unsupportable. What's achieved in draft 9 is a firm structure. Although the exact wording (even the end words) will vary before she's through, the architecture—the development of the argument within the refrain—is secured and will not, from here on out, be doubted:

stanza 1: willingness "to be lost" residing within things;
stanza 2: first imperative and "usual list" ("Lose something everyday"—keys, glasses);
stanza 3: second imperative and return to metaphor of the title ("Practice losing . . .");
stanza 4: intensified tone ("Look!") and increased value of lost items (mother's watch, houses);
stanza 5: "vaster losses" (cities, a continent).

It seems not farfetched to think that this structural solidity and the arc of the steadily torqued tone precipitate another timely arch, the first promising sketch of a final stanza:

> All that I write is false, it's evident
> The art of losing isn't hard to master.
> oh no.
> [anything] at all anything but one's love. (Say it: disaster.)

Something is *solved there* with Bishop's characteristic parenthesis. It enables a return of the hard-nosed, intrusive voice of draft 1 (also parenthetical) which articulates the other side—the underside—of the paradox, and its appearance supplies a crucial structural piece, clarified in the immediate adjustment written and crossed out in draft 10, restored in 11:

> The art of losing wasn't hard to master
> with this exception. (*Write it*.) Write "disaster".

and then stewed over in draft 12:

> the art of losing wasn't too hard to master
> with this exception. (Stupid! Write!)
>   (*Write it!*) this disaster.
> except this loss (*Oh, write it!*) this disaster.

but this loss is (Go on: write it!) is [seems] disaster.

This art of losing wasn't too hard to master
in general, but [t]his (Oh, write it!)   seems
in general, but this (Oh go on! Write it!) looks like disaster.
but this (Oh go on! Write it!) seems disaster.
doesn't (oh isn't it) it does look like disaster—

By draft 13, the stutter is secured, italics and quotation marks replaced by extended syntax and alliteration, a return of the recurrent "L" of "lose," "losing," "lost," "last," "lovely," and "love":

even if this [when it] looks like (Write it!) like disaster.

Now again revision becomes purposeful, still focused on tone, the remaining drafts seeming to work backward from that authority. As if to establish the ground to be violated by the interruption, the changes in the refrain (drafts 13 and 14) move away from assertion and certainty toward ambivalence:

the loss of love is possible to master,
            . . . something one must master
            . . . not too hard to master . . .

Meanwhile, after Bishop restores, in draft 10, the specific "you" of the initial draft, there is a similar movement in diction:

But, losing you (eyes of the Azure Aster)
And losing you now (a special voice, a gesture)
            . . . (a funny voice . . . the joking voice)

What remains unresolved, however, and stubborn, is the exact amount of self-knowledge in the controlling voice. Draft 10's "I've written lies above" is changed in pencil to "above's all lies," the two phrases then alternating with "I wrote a lot of lies" through five reworkings of the stanza on draft 11—surviving in some form, that is, until its outright contradiction: in 12, "above's *not* lies" [my italics] and then, through four re-workings, "I haven't lied above"; in 13, "doesn't mean I've lied [I'm lying]"; in 14, "these are not lies" (by hand). Meanwhile, each typed version, drafts 9 through 13, makes some small change to the wording of the first five stanzas—final editorial adjustments concomitant with the large-scale wrestling with the conclusion.

A carbon of Vassar draft 15 is what Bishop sent to Frank Bidart for his response, but she was still fiddling with that closure. (See figure 2.)

His notes duplicate the changes, written by hand in the original, which she dictated to him over the telephone: "further" made "farther," in stanza 3; a dash to introduce stanza 6 ("—Even losing you . . ."); "the" instead of "a" joking voice in that same line; and perhaps more significantly, elimination of the one full repetition of X, the villanelle's usually variant middle rhyme—a change, in line 2, from "so many things seem really meant/to be lost" to

> so many things seem filled with the intent
> to be lost that their loss is no disaster.

Maybe this small accommodation at the poem's opening simply diverted the poet's gaze long enough for a corrected final stanza to shimmer in peripheral vision. Or maybe the addition of another L-word ("filled") to the torqued enjambment of line 2, without subsequent caesura, suggested a solution for closure as well. In any case, the fluster at the penultimate moment recorded by Bishop's hand on the Vassar draft—"may not" (scratched through) "I still do [can't] [won't] lie"—finds resolution during the conversation with Bidart: annotating the typescript ("these are not lies"), his notes first replace "are" with "were," then restore "are," and then enter "I shan't have lied," a grammatical shift that nails the tone with future perfect tense.

The new helping verb, one should note, is placed in a position of stress, making a half-rhyme on the stable *b* end sound (intent, meant, went, shan't), and marks an elevation in diction exactly counter to the movement toward idiom characteristic of all the other changes in the stanza. In that sense, it is an almost purely technical solution, but one that embod-

[Draft 15]

ONE ART

The art of losing isn't hard to master:
so many things seem ~~really to be meant.~~ intent   filled with the intent
to be lost that their loss is no disaster.

Lose something every day. Accept the fluster
of lost door-keys, the hour badly spent.
The art of losing isn't hard to master.

Then practice losing farther, losing faster:
places, and names, and where it was you meant
to travel. None of these will bring disaster.

I lost my mother's watch. And look! my last, or
next-to-last of three loved houses went.
The art of losing isn't hard to master.

I lost two cities, lovely ones. And, vaster,
some realms I owned, two rivers, a continent.
I miss them, but it wasn't a disaster.

— Even losing you (a joking voice, a gesture
I love) these ~~are~~ not lies. It's evident
the art of losing's not too hard to master
though it may look like (Write it!) like disaster.

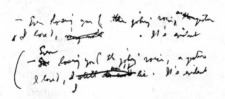

figure 2

ies, within the tightly orchestrated music of the L-verbs (losing/love/
lied) and long vowel (*I* love, *I* shan't, have *lied*), the tension between form
and idiom—and, thereby, between inconvenience and assault, irritation
and grief, mastery and disaster. And when it occurs, pushing the dramatic
occasion into an imagined completed future, the emotional dilemma and
the poem's true subject—anticipatory, unbearable dread—is suddenly,
horribly clarified.

The question Bidart remembers Bishop asking was whether it strayed
too far from spoken idiom. His reassurance must have been sufficient, for
the new phrase had already been added when the poem was set in type
on April 26, 1976, six months after Millier dates the first draft, to recapitu-
late and just sufficiently overstate the ironic argument:

> —Even losing you (the joking voice, a gesture
> I love) I shan't have lied. It's evident
> the art of losing's not too hard to master
> though it may look like (*Write it!*) like disaster.

Now what bridges the gulf into the final quatrain is one last moment of
dignified composure before heartbreak erupts from underground. How
account for that last crucial revision—Dionysian, an unstoppable contin-
uation of the direct emotion ("gesture/I love") acknowledged openly, finally, in draft 14? Apollonian, derivative of the formal choice of severe
enjambment, late caesura, alliteration? Occasioned by biographical circumstance, something Alice did or said, some small achievement in that
autumn's struggle with booze? Prompted by a suggestion from Frank Bidart over the phone? All of the above? The point remains: it took Bishop
fifteen distinct drafts, and another several dozen alterations thereon, and
long deep thought in musical language, and impressive tenacity, to arrive
there, there being precise feeling and felt intelligence.

A long way from the Hollywood studio, but not that far, finally, from
Coleridge in his study:

In Shakespeare's poems the creative power and the intellectual energy wrestle as in
a war embrace. Each in its excess of strength seems to threaten the extinction of the
other. . . . What then shall we say? even this: that Shakespeare, no mere child of na-

ture; no automaton of genius; no passive vehicle of inspiration possessed by the spirit, not possessing it; first studied patiently, meditated deeply, understood minutely, till knowledge, become habitual and intuitive, wedded itself to his habitual feelings, and at length gave birth to that stupendous power. . . .

—*Biographia Literaria*

ROBERT MICHAEL PYLE

Secrets of the Talking Leaf

[PORT TOWNSEND WRITERS' CONFERENCE]

The befuddlement of native peoples upon encountering European adventurers stemmed from many unfamiliarities. There were the carved and shiny sticks that thundered and brought blood. There were bright beads and blankets of unknown materials. There were metals that would easily rend flesh or wood. And perhaps as perplexing as anything, there were the clusters of white leaves with marks upon them that seemed to speak. At least, when the interlopers looked at the leaves, they spoke in words that seemed to arise from the clusters. Messages, dictates, deeds, and treaties ripe for breaking all were carried on single large leaves that could be rolled or folded. Whole philosophies were borne in bunches of leaves called books. Talking leaves appeared to carry great power, for they might signify concord or war, beneficence or confiscation, salvation, deportation, or death, depending upon the marks; and sometimes, they moved men to raise their arms aloft and tell of gods.

Sequoyah, a young man of the Tennessee Cherokee, was not the only Indian to wonder over the power of the leaves that talked. But he was the only one to do something about it.

In 1969, I worked as a ranger-naturalist in Sequoia National Park in California's Sierra Nevada. Sequoia, the second-oldest national park in North America, protects the most massive trees in the world—the giant sequoias. Their relatives, the coast redwoods, are the tallest trees in the world and many of the ones that remain reside in Redwood National Park in the coastal lowlands of California. When I went to lead nature walks and give campfire programs among the Big Trees, I had no idea where the name sequoia came from. I assumed it was Indian, of Californian origin. Looking back, it seems surprising that none of the evening programs, guided walks, or interpretive exhibits told the story of Sequoyah in depth. But then, perhaps not so surprising: his was a radical, even deeply revolutionary act; and 1969 was the summer when a hundred mounted rangers with truncheons raided Yosemite Meadows, cracking hippie heads in a display of fervor that mimicked that of Chicago police at the Democratic National Convention a year earlier.

Sequoyah was born in Tennessee two hundred years before, and later transported to Arkansas. He noticed the capacities given whites by their peculiar talking leaves. His tribesmen were divided in their theories: some thought books were conferred by a god who denied them, like so many other things, to their people, thus proving the depressing rightness of European supremacy. Others believed that writing had nothing to do with gods, but was the invaders' own invention. Sequoyah was one of these. Convinced that this tool was within his own reach, he pondered the question and, eventually, worked it out. Using a direct syllabic notation of his own invention, he brought literacy to his people in a remarkably short time and changed their lives.

The wonderfully evocative term "talking leaves" gave the title for Craig Lesley's fine anthology of Native American short stories (Dell, 1992). Reading this stunning collection, we see that the secret exposed by Sequoyah has become abundantly owned by the first people at last.

The technical knowledge of a written language, of course, is only the first step in allowing the leaves to truly speak. If all it took to make literature was the ability to write in any given tongue, we would not distinguish between the literary arts and the telephone book. In fact, this is a curious distinction between writing and the other arts: most of the members of many cultures possess the raw materials, since basic literacy is taken for granted as an everyday survival skill like simple math, or telling directions or time. This means that just about anyone is capable of writing up a storm. Yet in art, prolific expression means little if it lacks the personal element that we variously call heart, soul, talent, spirit. Many are given to write; few, to really Write.

To allow the leaves to speak: that is the task. I often tell students that we should aspire to be amanuenses to the land: to let the land speak (in all its voices: human and otherwise), then take dictation, and try to get some of the words right. "How do you know when you get the words right?" they ask.

"You know," I reply. When we do, the leaves not only speak; they positively sing.

But your right words will not be mine. Words are all names for something, and names are as relative as the rain: one minute a downpour, the next more virga, evaporating before it hits the ground, the rain shifts substance and meaning before our eyes. Names, and all words (mere symbols after all), do the same. Listen to the names given the great trees of the Sierra Nevada, for instance. We call them giant sequoias, naming them for their massiveness and their genus, which in turn was named to celebrate a man who performed a giant task. But the botanists have since changed the genus, separating the redwoods into three genera: *Sequoia* now belongs to species *sempervirens* alone, the coast redwood. *Metasequoia* takes in the sole species *glyptostroboides*, the dawn redwood, known only as an extinct fossil species until discovered in living verdure in a Chinese monastery during World War II. As for the giant redwoods, they have been consigned to the new genus *Sequoiadendron*, meaning sequoia tree. Fair enough: *Sequoiadendron gigantea*, known to all as the Big Trees of California. But what were the native names for the largest trees in the world? We can be sure they did not call the biggest one the General Sherman Tree, as we do.

And how are these monoliths known elsewhere, in the arboreta of invading nations, where they might be grown alongside botanical booty such as Douglas fir, Lewisia, Clarkia, Franklinia, and other living souvenirs of Manifest Destiny? When I lived in England, I often saw the crowns of giant sequoias in their first hundred years, poking through the morning mists, mimicking the village spires. "What are those trees?" I once asked a passing vicar.

"Why," he responded, as if to a simpleton, "they are Wellingtonias, of course! Everyone knows that."

Sequoyah taught a people to master the exclusive tool of their oppressors. The Duke of Wellington defeated Napoleon at Waterloo. Both were honored for their Herculean feats by having their handles tacked onto the biggest trees in the world. (Sequoyah also got the national park, and Wellington, a type of rubber boot.) So it happened that the names of a Native American lexicographer and a British warrior both came to convey a tree that has nothing to do with either one of them.

As naturalists know, it has been anything but uncommon for the so-called discoverers of new species of plants and animals—or anyone they wished to patronize, acclaim, commemorate, or flatter—to carry the names of those organisms into scientific perpetuity. Interestingly, the taxonomist who gives an animal or plant its scientific name is known as its "author," as if the act of bestowing the Linnaean binomial appellation of genus and species were tantamount to breathing life itself into the organism. Not to put too fine a point on this, systematists are rarely Frankensteinian in their presumption. Among the gentlest of people, they are truly enamored of the creatures they attend to, as befits the practitioners of Adam's task.

Even so, the classifiers are possessed of all the venality, envy, whimsy, and ego that beset the rest of us, and the names they give often show it. Butterflies, a group I know fairly well, betray in their names every imaginable motive. Because early lepidopterists frequently boasted classical educations, they felt compelled to use them. So it is that the names of many swallowtails commemorate heroes of the Trojan Wars, while arctic fritillaries bear the names of Norse goddesses and their more southerly cousins embody mythic figures such as Cybele, Aphrodite, and Hippolyta. From the number of fauns, satyrs, nymphs, and other Greek and Roman rustic deities found among butterfly checklists, you could be forgiven for thinking that these insects live a constant bacchanal of drinking and mating—and that is, in fact, the case. Yet the observant authors of our butterflies did not always draw their monikers from the European cultural canon. The names of American skippers, for example, include many Native American designations: Hobomok, Pochahontas, Sachem, Ottoe, Pawnee, Dakota, Pahaska, Delaware, Zabulon—often inhabiting the same grasslands and woodlands where their namesakes once roamed.

Nineteenth-century explorer-naturalists, in need of financial backing for their collecting expeditions, named finds for sponsors or patrons, such as the genus of giant moths called *Rothschildia* after the financier-naturalist. Lord Rothschild bestowed as well as received patronyms, naming the largest butterfly in the world Queen Alexandra's Birdwing. The New Guinea giant spreads a foot in wingspan, and the first female was collected with a shotgun. Alexandra, the much-beloved Queen Consort of Edward VII, had received an earlier dash of immortality when the influential Philadelphia lepidopterist W. H. Edwards named Queen Alexandra's Sulphur for her in 1863, upon her marriage to the Prince of

Wales. Edwards named another brilliant western sulphur after Theodore Mead. An enterprising youth who hoped for Edith Edwards's hand, Mead went forth by stagecoach and rail to bring back butterfly novelties to her father. One of these was a bright copper butterfly, prettier than any bauble, that has ever since worn Edith's name. She, in turn, became Edith Mead. Apparently, Mead got the words right.

Two books I am working on have brought me nose to nose with striking examples of viewpoint in choosing the words, again the names of butterflies. For a Colorado novel with a Magdalenian subtext, I looked into the derivation of the name of a completely black mountain species known as the Magdalena Alpine. Was this a devotional gesture by a devout Roman Catholic butterfly hunter? I asked F. Martin Brown, the late historian of Western butterfly study. "Absolutely not!" Brownie replied. It seems that Herman Strecker, the insect's author, was irreligious, and missed no opportunity to embarrass his best friend, a parson. So he named the most undistinguished and obscure moth he could find, *Jehovah*; and the sooty-winged *Erebia magdalena* was no doubt named to rub his friend's nose in the saint's supposedly besmirched reputation.

The other example also has religious overtones. A colleague in New York performed a revision of a group of small Western forest butterflies called cedar hairstreaks. At the time he was a follower of the Reverend Sun Myung Moon, and he named several new species after prominent Moonies—this to the chagrin of local lepidopterists, since we will be stuck with this inapt nomenclature ever after.

More recently, the same lepidopterist has assisted me in compiling a collection of the late novelist Vladimir Nabokov's butterfly writings for a Beacon Press edition. Many know of Nabokov's interest in butterflies, but few realize the depth of his passion for them or that he was a notable lepidopterist in his own right. My New York friend has lately been completing some of the taxonomic tasks that Nabokov began, by naming many new species of the small butterflies known as Blues that Nabokov had studied and loved. But now, having renounced the Moonies, my friend is mining the master's oeuvre for truly Nabokovian labels for the hitherto nameless butterflies. I am happy to say that these lovely Latin American Blues will bear such delightful and suitable names as *Nabokovia ada*, *Itylos pnin*, and *Madeleinea lolita*.

What have the names of butterflies to do with the craft of fine writing?

No more or less than the words we use for worms, or rather the worms we use for words. Consider, for a moment, the way worms worm their way through our lexicon. We say (in an inaccuracy that Nabokov the scientist-wordsman would never have countenanced) that butterflies come from worms, and butterflies are commonly employed (to the point of cliché, such as Nabokov the great symbolist would never have used) as a symbol for resurrection. Thus, with only one layer of removal, we link worms with immortality. Yet worms are the very agent of decay in every lore (though we really mean maggots): "The worms go in, the worms go out. . . ." With one word, however twisted from its actual meaning, we manage to convey the entire range of existence from birth to rot to rebirth. And the only thing that makes our meaning clear is context: "worm" on its own conveys nothing.

Rather, nothing that we can agree upon. Three examples of worm usage make the point that each of us brings his or her own baggage or bias to the lesson of any given talking leaf, at least until we listen enough to put it in context. First, consider Charles Darwin. This graceful writer's last and, according to Stephen Jay Gould, his loveliest book is entitled *The Formation of Vegetable Mould Through the Action of Worms* (1882). It describes the very evolution of the landscape in terms of lowly wormworks. Darwin watched worms all his life and admired their industry, behavior, and adaptability immensely. When he heard the term "worm," he thought good things. Second, think of the right-wing Uncle Sam billboard along Interstate 5, between Seattle and Portland, guaranteed to be more reactionary than thou on any issue. During the Iraqi invasion, the board's owner asked whether we would be bombing Baghdad if there were spotted owls there and compared Saddam Hussein to a "human worm." That was the worst thing he could think to say about Hussein. One of these authors, a British naturalist, revered the word worm and all it implied to him. The other, a Washington turkey farmer, reviled it. You could easily find similarly diametric views over the words bat, moth, cricket, or football.

Now consider a third specific use of the same word, this time in context. When Wallace Stegner lectured in Seattle several years ago, he summed the writer's task by challenging us to "leave the worms of wonder working in the mind of the reader." Was this a positive or a negative reading of the name? The idea of "worms working in the mind" clearly evokes the vicarious discomfort of imagined decay, inspiring a squeamish tickle.

Yet by coupling "worm" with "wonder," Stegner deftly twists the sensation toward the positive, even the rapturous. After all, what feels better (to a reader) than wonderment—even riding on worms—twisting its way through the dumbed-down convolutions of our day-numbed brains?

Now we come to the hard, clear relationship between the secret of the leaves that talk and the irresistible human penchant to give names. A name—a word—sitting on its own can convey anything to anyone, depending on personal history, bias, phobia, obsession, experience, association, or whim. Yet surrounded by others, words take root in the soil of context: not fixed, nor bereft of shifting nuance, translucent layer, or alternative meanings (just read Nabokov!), but freed from the footloose shiftlessness of the uprooted rune. Like an animal in a zoo cage or a plant in a pot with no hint of habitat, a word on its own can convey nothing beyond its own hide. But as soon as you stick things together—the way you found them in the wild or in some new combo—you get an ecology. Interactions become inevitable. Togetherness of words forces not only context, but also cadence, collaboration, and color, assonance and dissonance, aim, attitude, and altitude. Sentences are family groups, and paragraphs are the neighborhoods they dwell within. Writing is indeed a community of words, and the author—not unlike the authors of the names of butterflies—is responsible for the organization of the living things within the habitat of the page.

Ultimately, then, getting the words right becomes a matter of responsibility. The botanist is responsible for the data that, properly transcribed, speak truly for the mute leaf pasted to the talking leaf of an herbarium sheet. So it is with us: as writers, we speak for that which cannot. Derelict in our duty, we run the risk of getting the data wrong. When that happens, the leaves lie . . . and the reader will always know. The secret of the talking leaves lies not with Gutenberg, nor with Sequoyah; no mere marks on a page can make what we call language. They give us the means alone, and from there on, we're on our own.

To help define where we are to go, I would like to take two quotations from Oregonian writer-friends and see how they cooperate. In the introduction to his sublime book *Having Everything Right*, Kim Stafford compares descriptive Kwakiutl names for places (such as the bay called "Insufficient Canoe," or the term for parts of an island separated by an isthmus at low tide: "Two round things meeting now and then") with bland Anglo names such as "courthouse" or "Vancouver." He invokes the term *hē'ladē*, meaning "having everything right," and says it could be "a portable name . . . it could be what we call earth. But it will not, unless we sift from our habits the nourishing ways: listening, remembering, telling, weaving a rooted companionship with home ground."

Barry Lopez, addressing the Pacific Northwest Booksellers' Association, enunciated a phrase that has haunted me ever since: he called us "the community of writers in service to readers."

Now, it seems to me that if writers were to rigorously seek a rooted companionship with home ground, so that their words and names carried the specificity and feeling of the Kwakiutl and the wit and humanity of a Stafford; and if readers were to recognize the service rendered by writers and reciprocate abundantly with their attentions, then we might at last have everything right: at least, much of what is important to writers—that is, notating the world exactly, and having someone appreciate it when we do.

Yet there are countervailing tendencies that detract from the prospects of our ever realizing *hē'ladē*. Let's take these in the reverse order from Lopez and Stafford's quotes, first looking at writers and readers, then coming back to the rooted companionship. In doing so we might be able to chisel our understanding of why we insist on defacing good clean leaves with our marks, and come to a clearer view of how we might at least do it better.

By some obvious measures, writers' service to readers does not seem to be a two-way thing. A tendency toward the devaluation of reading and the displacement of the book as a major cultural form have literary people worried. The field marks can be easily listed: (*a*) takeovers of independent publishers by multinational corporations and a narrowed focus on the bottom line as a result; (*b*) the inventory tax, an amazing American manifestation of philistinism, one of the most punitive anti-intellectual devices anywhere, leading to a restructuring of the publishing industry with small printings, early remainderings, and a big fat out-of-print sign as its hallmarks; (*c*) the rise of ignoble book-barns, where books are units and writing is product and the resemblance to a real bookstore with informed staff and concern with authors is largely and insidiously ersatz; (*d*) a declining readership for serious fiction, poetry, and belles lettres; (*e*) a growing readership for instant oatmeal such as *Bridges of Madison County* and the strident belchings of Rush Limbaugh and glitzy city fables and violent scary thrillers and international plot plots and angel-fakery and sub-pop psychobabble and cartoons and manuals for successful self-preening, self-aggrandizement, self-abasement, self-absorption, and self-promotion; (*f*) the much-heralded onslaught of the CD-ROM with its interactive alternative to mere talking leaves; the much-ballyhooed information interstate with its invisible substitutes for print; and their supposed outcome, the much-exaggerated inevitability of the death of the book.

Why, you might well ask, should anyone persist in writing for traditional publication in the face of all this? Are we not merely indulging a romantic form of onanism, stubbornly sticking by a dying idyll? Are we to be thought of as bull-headed Luddites, for maintaining our loving involvement with paper, print, and all things bookish? Do we poetize in vain, draw characters for oblivion, essay our way into anonymity? So it might seem, as the community of writers scribbles pointlessly away into the autumn of the talking leaf.

And yet, we write on: because remunerative or not, a book to us is something that we love and aspire to woo. To make the leaves speak sweetly—that is the siren. This is not to say that the pleasures and satisfactions of the scrivener cannot be had from disk to screen, skipping committal to the printed page. But to know and love the book is a devotion that will never (in the hearts and minds of many) be replaced by any image romanced from an optical screen by bits, bytes, bleeps, and pixels. Just as it has often been observed that curling up with a terminal will never take the place of a cat, a cup of cocoa, and a book, so will the "publication" of work by electronic means—a marvelous thing in itself—never satisfy the same part of the soul that thrills to share itself in the same medium known by Chaucer and Shakespeare, Colette and Saki, Margaret Wise Brown and Toni Morrison.

When Robert Frost traveled, he took with him the entirety of Bennett Cerf's Modern Library, in great wooden cases that he had delivered to his rooms so that he could select whichever volume he wished to take to bed. He could have had the same thing today from a single digital disk, and had pictures and voices and music to boot. Why do I imagine that he would not have been amused to open his crate and find a CD-ROM lurking in place of his books?

Books will change, of that there is no doubt. Electronic publishing was the hottest topic at the recent American Book Association meeting, and the rights surrounding it are blowing a maelstrom among publishers and the Authors Guild. There will be fewer paper books published, for sure. Yet is that all bad for book lovers? Who would not agree that there is too much published today? The birchwoods of the northern taiga are being raided for pulp to fill our mailboxes with tripe, our newspapers with advertisers, and our bookshelves with dross. If much of this can go on instantly erasable screens, how much better for trees, for mail carriers, and for real books, which might again emerge from the crowd.

After all, when big business swallows honored but weak old publishing houses, small new vibrant ones have a way of arising. Fine printing and bookmaking are alive and well, and may come into their own again as mass-produced books diminish. Literary publishing is like a balloon: push it or squeeze it in one place, and it pops up in another. There is a resiliency to Gutenberg's trade. And, if the info-boosters were to be proven right and new books did drop out of the picture, perhaps it would be a favor in disguise. We bibliophiles could retreat to the second-hand stores and the ruins of the libraries, and maybe we could actually achieve that elusive and gossamer goal of all readers: to catch up.

In the end, the reasons that books as we know them and writers as we know ourselves will persist are at least two: first, because (in whatever diluted numbers) there will continue to be curious, educated people who love to read, for whom reading means a book. Second, because a book, though removed from the author by editor, printer, the page and its glyphs, is still, held in the hands and perused and put down and picked up and referred to and lent and retrieved and dog-eared and smelling and dog-chewed and flapping on the porch in a breeze like unruly leaves on a bush, something real—a physical object in a way that evanescent images on a screen can never be. An experience with a book is a direct experience. Many people obviously find experiences with computer screens to be real, intense, and satisfying. But it is a different kind of experience: it may be interactive, but it is not interactive with the world. For writers, most of whom spend way too much time in the company of computers as it is, fondling a physical book is like taking a walk: it is a sensory oasis.

When I am asked how I can live without television, e-mail, Internet, fax, an answering machine, call-waiting, CD-ROM, etc., I say, "Easy. Why in the world would I want to live even more of my life in front of a screen than I already do? And what sort of input do I really need that I can't find in a good library, a good bookstore, and out of doors in a perfectly good world?"

"But the *information* you lose," they go on. To which I reply that in my view, writers are inundated with information. The very last thing in the world that I want, next to Hantavirus, is more *incoming*. Why did writers' retreats evolve, anyway?

And it is this question that brings us back to our second quotation. When Kim Stafford speaks of weaving "a rooted companionship with home ground," he is invoking us to find time and attention and care for direct experience of the world around us. If there is a shallowness and vapidity to a lot of what passes for writing, it is because TV, The Great Presence of the second half of this century, and other amusements and distractions, have seduced us away from a one-on-one with the dirt and the air and our neighbors, and we have forgotten how to perceive them, let alone interact with them and report on them honestly and vividly. Nor do we have a clue what we ourselves are (hence the success of all the self-self books) in relation to the world around us. That makes it impossible to write personally. And writing that is not personal is copy fit for telephone books.

I cannot refer to telephone books without mentioning my friend and neighbor Carlton Appelo, who is also president of the Western Wahkiakum Telephone Company. A fine writer and local historian, Carlton employs the annual telephone directories as repositories for his moving accounts of our local pioneers and their vanished communities. Owner of a captive audience, Carlton Appelo is the only writer I know who makes the telephone book work as a medium of literature. Most of us lack such an outlet and must make do with the traditional homes for personal print.

As terminal writers who wish not to be extensions of our terminals, we can resist a world that seems bent on becoming less literary and more removed from the personal, direct response. Some of the ways are simple to voice if not always to perform. Live directly. Allow your knowledge, sensation, and experience to draw from the physical surfaces of things. Take at least some of your satisfaction from outside of your brain and its attendent machines, every day. Every day, come to your senses—use every one of them at every opportunity. In seeking to serve readers, be one yourself: read widely, abundantly, diversely, demandingly, critically, lightheartedly, generously, without excuse, and more than you ever thought possible. And when it comes time to make your own leaves speak, do so from your own carefully observed, individually encountered experience, in as much particularity of detail as you can possibly recount.

Spend gladly as much time as it takes to get the words right. As William Shawn of the *New Yorker* told John McPhee, "It takes as long as it takes." Read it to someone, to yourself, to your cat, then do it all over again. All of this is proof against a world where literary expression threatens to vanish into nothing more than the speed of light.

As John McPhee told me, he answers all of his correspondence, by hand. He asks how could he do otherwise, when the letters he receives are the one actual sign of a bond between the writer and his readers? To live as writers, we must revise our expectations of reward. Few will make their livelihood exclusively or even substantially through their writing, and to expect to do so is probably asking for disappointment and disillusionment. But to pay the occasional light bill or car payment with a writing check is not unreasonable, and viewed in that light, every tangible reward brings jubilation. Nor should we live or die based on reviews or acclaim. As writer Susan Lardner said in the *New Yorker*, "A good writer has no reason to be surprised when the world offers him less in the way of fame and riches than he deserves." Expect calumny and neglect: then if praise comes, it too will be a delight and a surprise.

Sometimes, just rewards jump up and surprise you. When I last taught here, many of us laughed along with Robert Olen Butler's remarkable fiction, and wrung our hands and towels with him when none of his five acclaimed novels were in print to be sold or signed alongside other faculty members' books. Some months later, I attended Bob's reading for his new book, *A Good Scent from a Strange Mountain*, at Elliott Bay Books in Seattle, along with five other souls. At dinner afterward, Bob told me that he didn't really mind because the six had been enthusiastic, but that it would be nice if this book were to bring more attention to the others, perhaps giving them a paperback future. A few months later, he won the Pulitzer Prize for Fiction.

This could happen to you; but it probably won't. It is enough to have those among us who flag the fact that literature lives, and is loved. That means a lot, and it lets us get on with our honorable task of scratching the letters on the leaves. And what, then, is the reward? If great remuneration is unlikely; if critical attention is sparse and praise even thinner on the ground, and if the publishing world we've read about and hoped or expected to join all our lives is changing under our feet like an ice-cream sidewalk in the sun, why bother?

Because of the possibility of achieving *hē'ladē*; or, if not having everything right, then getting enough of the words right that you know you've made something that looks good, reads well, and will stand. As the Blackfeet singer-songwriter Jack Gladstone wrote in his song "The Builder," "You know, building is a risky thing to do / When the work you perform outlasts you." Jack also wrote, in a splendid song entitled "Dyin' for a Metaphor," "That's why we're designed to weave our way / Through the forest of word-lore / Dyin' for a metaphor." These things are true of us, the writers, who are builders. And when we find our way through the forest of word-lore with just the right metaphor, and know that we have built something that will outlast us, we take great joy.

And for the same reason that John McPhee answers all his mail. Malcolm Cowley said, "A writer is someone with readers." When you know that you have a reader, one who took time to read your stuff from among all the stuff that's out there, one who chose you over the screen and other cheap thrills, and one who has gone to the trouble of expressing love for your work in a letter, it is worth more than any review or royalty check. At least, it is worth a great deal.

The *New Yorker* recently profiled James Wilcox, a novelist with five well-reviewed books to his name who is nonetheless living in near penury. James Stewart's article closed with a letter Wilcox received from one devoted reader, a pregnant woman whose father had just suffered a heart attack and who couldn't sleep in the heat. In part, she wrote: "I'm clutching to the things that I love. And I love your books . . . please write another novel fast because I can't sleep. . . . Is that a lot to ask? I'd do the same for you."

Such are the real rewards. If not a letter from someone sleeplessly awaiting your words, it might be a comment from a workmate, unsolicited praise from a partner, or a kind word from someone who accidentally picked up your story, thinking it was a recipe. Even an unkind word. Anything to prove that you have broken through the incandescent screen to connect with another human, that you got enough of the words right to make the talking leaves shimmer and rustle in the breeze. When that faint whisper shouts above the cacophony of the information gridlock, not only for yourself but for someone else, then you know why you write, and you know that writing (and all it means) will never die as long as literate creatures litter the landscape, committing senseless and random acts of reading.

I am currently completing a long project inspired by the rich and many Bigfoot traditions. One of the schisms I have found among the true believers is that between those who would kill a Sasquatch to prove its existence and those who don't think it's worth skirting the moral brink to do so. When I recently interviewed Dr. Grover Krantz on this point, the Washington State University anthropologist and Bigfoot seeker said that if he had a chance to pull the trigger it would be the hardest decision of his life, and he would regret either outcome as long as he lived. But he believes that the discovery and subsequent protection would warrant the life taken. When I asked him about the morality of killing a possible hominid, he said that the animal's apparent lack of tools renders it not human, from an anthropological viewpoint. Many other serious searchers agree with that opinion. Language, of course, is considered more advanced than tool use, and many Northwest Indian traditions speak of Bigfoot as having language. Whether the animal exists corporeally or metaphorically, it is a powerful presence. Yet its seeming lack of tools, fire, and talk makes it liable to be shot to prove its existence.

Perhaps this would indeed lead to ultimate protection, and one hesitates in any case to make comparisons between human ethics and the metaphysics of monsters. After all, if Grendel walked today, he would not exactly be embraced by the ACLU, munching the heads of Thanes being a capital crime. Yet it is instructive to remember that many episodes of imperial genocide were justified on the basis that the victims were savages, who did not even possess language. Of course they all did, often languages whose subtlety and range of expression surpassed that of their conquerers. Yet, lacking a written language, they were dismissed as sub-intelligent. And because they had not mastered the secrets of the talking leaf, they were powerless to combat violent change through the power of the pen. Not that it would have been enough: Edward Bulwer-Lytton's quotation, after all, reads in full: *"Beneath the rule of men entirely great,* the pen is mightier than the sword." That's a big if. Even so, Sequoyah recognized the advantage given the whites by books and other documents, and he believed that it was obtainable.

In search of the pen's power, he went into the woods deliberately and pondered the problem. Twelve years later, he emerged not with a *Walden*, but with the means to make one: the only syllabic alphabet ever perfected in its entirety by an individual. The literacy he was able rapidly to bestow upon his people led to the eventual confederation of the Cherokee Nation after removal to Oklahoma. When Sequoyah joined treaty talks in Washington, D.C., he was asked why he had made his written language. Jeremiah Evarts wrote this contemporary account of his reply:

> He had observed that many things were found out by men, and known in the world, but that this knowledge escaped and was lost, for want of some way to preserve it. He had also observed white people write things on paper, and he had seen books; and he knew that what was written down remained and was not forgotten. He had attempted, therefore, to fix certain marks for sounds, and thought that if he could make certain things fast on paper, it would be like catching a wild animal and taming it.

Sequoyah was right. What is written down is not forgotten. It is powerful, and it can change everything. It is also all we have.

Between Two Silences

I am partly to blame for the title of this panel: "The Year My Voice Broke Through." I am not so sure about "The Year" part because it seems to me a Voice is always breaking through. But a Voice does "break through," and what it breaks through is the writer. In the process, the struggle defines both the Voice and the writer.* In an interview in the *Paris Review*, the poet Anne Sexton said, "The poetry is often more advanced, in terms of my unconscious, than I am." The same can be said of a Voice. I often feel my poems are larger than I am, and the characters are more courageous. My work is dominated by tough, intelligent women who won't take shit from anyone, much less a man. I am beginning to think that "finding your Voice" means getting used to being bossed around.

Looking at it another way, I think finding your Voice means choosing your angels. The word "angel" comes from the Greek *angelos*, or messenger. My own angels, Margaret, Annie, and more recently, Mad Anne arrive with messages from the self. They have a woman's clear sense of men, and an ironic, critical "take" on the world. Being women, they get past the perceptions of men. But even when they are talking about themselves, they are indirectly talking about what the world of men is or is not, and therefore, about me.

These days I am writing in a male Voice close to my own. It is "hard sledding" writing from the *self* when our society seems bent on writing off the Voice of entire classes of individuals. Seniors are told they have used

---

*Due to time constraints it is not possible to consider the relationship between "voice" and "vision" in this presentation, issues of vision being another much neglected subject in the discourse on contemporary writing.

up their quota of services and ought to make way for the young, whose lives are more valuable. Youth are told they can't read, can't write, and there are no jobs for them. In the vernacular of adults with day jobs, youth are no longer the hope of tomorrow, but a problem to be solved. And because they have been reminded of their marginality so often, Youth, and many other groups, believe it. They have been shut out of today and shut out of tomorrow.

At a seminar in Regina recently, Gary Geddes quoted John Ciardi, who said a poem is "a countermotion across a silence." That is, of course, one level on which a Voice occurs and one level of silence. But there is another silence as well, The Big Silence:

> The Big Silence is the highest child poverty rate in Canada,
>   which we of the New Jerusalem failed to notice until
>   1989.

> The Big Silence is diabetes melitis among Indian people,
>   which we in the home of "too many doctors," discovered
>   "shockingly," a few months ago in the *Leader Post*.

> It is the headcount of 17: 17, the wake of secondary victims left
>   by every pathological gambler in Slot Machine Hell.

> The Big Silence is the dashed vision, the low road, "leave it to
>   Janice, leave it to Roy"*
> It is co-optation
> The Big Silence is Delay, Delay Delay
> The Big Silence is the hole in mental health
> The hole in education
> The hole in a seniors policy
> The hole in equality
> The hole in justice
> The Big Silence is the hole in front of your job
> The Big Silence is the hole in your self-respect

*Janice McKinnon, Saskatchewan's Minister of Finance, and Saskatchewan Premier, Roy Ramanow.

The Big Silence is the hole in Leo LaChance*
The Big Silence is denial, the gauze on your eyes, the words
  squeezed back in our throats
And it is all one
The Big Silence is The Big Silence

That was what the Sage Hill poets would call a "slow rant." It talks
about the culture of denial, and it talks about losses. In the context of today's panel, it raises the problem of the marginalized Voice of the poet,
which is a special case of the marginalization of all Voices. John Ciardi
speaks of one kind of silence, an interior one. As a poet, living in the world,
I am caught between two silences: Ciardi's silence and The Big Silence.
This is where I am positioned. It is where my Voice is now.

Where does the Voice come from? There is no simple answer. I do not believe a writer has a single Voice, but many Voices which "break through"
at different times.

Samuel Johnson said, "What is written without effort is in general read
without pleasure."

I do not believe this. First, I can think of no real writer who writes
"without effort." Second, the common experience of writers is that work
which comes quickly often stands up to work that has been slaved over,
cussed at, and made to sleep downstairs with the dog.

I tend to write long poems. For some time, I rarely wrote anything under a page long. Some of my characters have given me quite long se-
quences. *Daniel* is composed entirely of characters speaking directly of
their experience at the moment they are living it. They invent their own
poetic vernacular to fit the moment, but their purpose is not poetry. Their
purpose is to speak. The poetry comes from the truth they have faced, or
failed to face, and from the human need to be heard which is the source
of these Voices.

Having the craft makes "finding your Voice" easier, but not easy.
"Craft" is not Voice, and the problem of finding new territory, of *how* to go

---

*Leo LeChance was an Indian killed in Prince Albert, Saskatchewan, by gun shop owner and
white supremacist, Carney Nerland—a notorious case resulting in an inconclusive inquiry into
the police investigation and white supremacist activities in the province.

deeper into the canyons of consciousness always remains. What really counts with Voice is boldness. As Anne Sexton said: "Fuck structure and grab your characters by the time balls. Each of us sits in our time; we're born, live and die."

Get into their lives, she says, and the poetry will take care of itself.

In his book *Leaping Poetry*, Robert Bly remarks that "rapid association"—or the "leaping" in poetry—is itself content and has a meaning that goes beyond language. I think of Voice in this way. Voice is content. An impulse which exists, even with the words stripped away.

An aspect of Voice, which I greatly admire in any kind of writing, is the impression of an individual imagination moving the work along in an almost physical way: this and the sense that the writer is discovering something that was not known until the moment it was written, a moment of revelation, or a flood of revelation. All this speaks not of technique, but of the deep learning which is necessary for good writing. By deep learning, I mean those things which are deeply true, knowledge the writer has to earn.

Not too long ago I heard Paul Wilson reading from his new book, *Dreaming My Father's Body*. In that book there is a poem called "Bathing Dad." There are other poems on the subject of grown children faced with the imminent death of a parent. "Bathing Dad" is also a poem about becoming a person. It is about how men in this culture fail to touch and about learning to touch. The son touches as he gives his father a sponge bath; the father, it is wished or implied (we aren't sure which), has at last learned to receive the touch; the sister present is touched as well, and this is another kind of touching. This is deep learning. And every so often, as in this poem, a Voice touches what our hands cannot.

One can hardly talk about Voice without bringing up the obvious—the oracular Voice in Tim Lilburn's poetry. In *Names of God*, there is a poem, "The Horses are Dying, Scotland 1920," where the horses stand before the North Sea:

> The visions sing: plunge in, plunge
> in, manes flying like spume.
> Plunge in you whom disease
> has driven to dream passionately
> of slaughter.

Tim is a vision-seeker, and this is how he seems to approach Voice: "... plunge in, plunge in." Like Jacob at the river, Lilburn has wrestled all night and wants to know that angel's name. "Let me go, for day is breaking," says the angel in the book of Genesis. "I will not let you go unless you bless me," replies Jacob, *choosing* his angel.

What is a Voice? A Voice is someone speaking, but maybe not. It is all definition through evasion. It may not be possible to define or understand a Voice. As Rilke said, "What is extraordinary and eternal does not want to be bent by us. . . ."

Many are silenced these days by what is outside us and in us. The visionless future is everywhere. Our heritage of struggle has been trivialized and is always referred to as part of the nostalgic past. We are struggling now for the future of our province, but who is there to proclaim it? Whose task is this, if not that of a writer. This conference is about the changing landscape of writing. I can only conclude that Saskatchewan's writing community will be asked to speak of the present, and to imagine a future in a way that the future has not been imagined in fifty years. Faced with this task, the purpose of our Voice is to make us strong and to prepare us for our work, for as Antonio Machado wrote:

> Mankind owns four things
> that are no good at sea.
> Anchor, rudder, oars,
> and the fear of going down.

X. J. KENNEDY

The Loneliness of the Writer

[WESLEYAN UNIVERSITY WRITERS' CONFERENCE]

I assume that to be a writer is to condemn oneself to some degree of loneliness, and that an ability to endure solitude—even to enjoy it—is part of any honest description of the writer's trade.

This sore truth first struck me when, in the early '70s, I found myself teaching in a short-lived educational experiment, at Tufts, called the College Within. The '60s had passed, but the College Within was a determined throwback to that grand era of communal living. Students did everything together: they studied in teams, they wrote collaborative reports and painted collaborative murals and even wrote collaborative poems. One student lobbied for a class in nude figure drawing, in which not only the model but all the artists ought to go nude, but as I recall, that suggestion was squelched by the director. When someone proposed that the college stage a Togetherness Festival, I felt bothered. Togetherness is all very well; I didn't deny the usefulness of communal effort; and yet somehow I felt that some valuable quality was being lost.

Those collaborative poems especially troubled me. Members of a group would contribute passages to an aggregate poem that unfolded right then and there, on the scene. No one would take responsibility for the quality of the poem, no one would stick out his or her neck and affix a by-line to the result. In my experience, poems weren't written by committees. Poems began in the memories and the feelings of one individual, and they took shape gradually, perhaps over a long time, in solitude. I wanted to urge, instead of that Togetherness Festival, a Solitude Festival, in which everybody would stop conversing, stop expending energy in talk, and instead go off and think and read books and write something in isolation. A motto for such a Solitude Festival seemed ready-made: Greta Garbo's line "I want to be alone."

Solitude, after all, has a respectable tradition. It seems a given that if you mean to become a prophet you'll spend some time in lonely meditation, confronting yourself, posing yourself ultimate questions. Jesus in the wilderness, Gautama Buddha under the bo tree, the Prophet Mohammed in his cave—these immortals retreated to the wilderness and, significantly, elected to return from it. In that wonderful chapter on solitude in *Walden*, Thoreau mocks the excesses of constant community: "I find it wholesome to be alone the greater part of the time. . . . We are for the most part more lonely when we go abroad among men than when we stay in our chambers."

I didn't dispute, back then as a college teacher, the value of communal effort, nor do I now. As a writer, I have collaborated with my wife, Dorothy, on textbooks and a children's book that required us to work over each other's prose. "Don't you fight?" we have been asked, and I must say we do— usually fruitfully. But somehow we haven't collaborated on poems, except in that I show Dorothy whatever I write and she points out things I haven't made clear. If this talk contains any practical advice for novice writers, it is this: Marry a critic whose judgment you trust.

Many in this audience are working journalists, and I daresay that writing in collaboration is familiar to you. How often a news story or a feature proves too large for a single reporter; and in how many newsrooms it is customary to work elbow-to-elbow with others. Reading about the life of H. L. Mencken lately, I learned that Mencken wrote much of his best work in a city room, producing columns and reportage so good that it has lasted as literature. But although he plied his typewriter amid the clamor of a news office, Mencken wrote as an individual. Some of his best essays are memoirs or autobiography or bits of personal opinion, forms of writing that don't invite collaboration. Brent Staples's recent *Parallel Time*, an account of growing up black in a white-dominated culture, had to be a one-man job.

Still more difficult to imagine is a poem written as a collaboration. Years ago Philip Dacey invited 102 other poets to write "The Great American Poem," a round-robin affair assembled by mail, with each poet contributing a single line. After six years in the making, the result was eventually printed in *Antaeus* for Winter 1979, but seems to have drawn only a passing flurry of attention, and not much praise. Each contributor tried to make it hard for the next contributor to go on, so that the poem reads like a series of jolting stops and starts. (When it came my turn, I couldn't resist rhyming my line with the one before it, producing a closed couplet that floated obstinately in a sea of free verse.) The only good poetry ever produced by a team may have been the King James Bible—and that was a translation.

In fiction, the chances for successful collaboration are only a little brighter. Decent novels have been produced by co-authors: Mark Twain and Charles Dudley Warner's *The Gilded Age* is a fairly impressive work; and the collaborations of Joseph Conrad and Ford Madox Ford, though less loudly acclaimed than what they wrote individually, are respectable. Early in the century, a collaborative novel, *The Whole Family*, sucked in the talents of Henry James, Edith Wharton, William Dean Howells, Mary E. Wilkins-Freeman, and others, but it didn't quite gel. Just the other year, Ken Kesey wrote a novel in collaboration with the members of his fiction-writing class. And yet—can you think of any really first-rate novel written by a pair, or a trio, or a team? I'm stumped, myself. Playwrights who have paired up seem to have come off better, as witness the teams of Beaumont and Fletcher, Thurber and Nugent, Kaufman and Hart. Shakespeare, scholars tell us, had a hand in *The Two Noble Kinsmen*, and yet when he wrote *Hamlet* and *Lear*, he worked alone.

My point is simply that, in literature, the fruits of solitude tend to surpass the fruits of community. You might now be thinking, All right, Kennedy, solitude is all very well, but *my* problem is to find time to be solitary. The strain of earning a living while at the same time writing—even more strenuous if you have kids—makes solitude scarce and hard-won.

This problem may be nearly universal, and writers have tried to solve it variously. One solution: Be an early riser. This method can be tried only by writers of great self-discipline. Victorian novelist Anthony Trollope is celebrated for that quality: with superhuman determination, he arose at the same time daily, and at 5:30 reread his output of the previous day. Then, with stopwatch before him, he proceeded to write 250 words every quarter hour from 6 until 8:30, when he went to his job in the post office. The poet Donald Hall, in a recent memoir, *Life Work*, tells us that he can hardly restrain himself until 4:30 in the morning when his day's work will begin. Hall and others have testified to the beauty and peacefulness of writing at dawn, before the rest of the world has roused. Sylvia Plath wrote the bulk of *Ariel* in early morning while her children were asleep— but, for Plath, solitude seems to have led not only to poetic triumph but to personal disaster. I haven't had much luck with early rising, myself— I've tried it, but found myself staring sleepily at a blank sheet of paper.

Another possible solution to the problem of finding solitude is to seize odd moments. Write now and again, in minutes rescued from your working day. William Carlos Williams was the master of such efficient use of time. As a pediatrician in East Rutherford, New Jersey, he would no sooner finish examining a baby than—bang! up would come a typewriter out of his fold-away desk and he would write for a few minutes until the next baby arrived. This method, too, is beyond me. I can't change records in my head that fast. Still, I've heard of a poet who writes while commuting to and from work, talking his compositions into a tape recorder.

Yet another solution is to discover a retreat that provides the solitude necessary. In Boston, there's The Writer's Room, which writers who need a place of refuge can apply to spend time in. But other public locales for work are possible, as young Ernest Hemingway demonstrated in his Paris café, writing short stories all day long. There exists a novel dedicated to a Manhattan cafeteria. Many writers attest to good luck from working in a public library. Somehow the spectacle of all those fellow bowed heads seems to induce concentration. Faulkner wrote *As I Lay Dying* while working the night shift in a power plant, which job required that every once in a while he throw on another shovelful of coal. Gary Snyder has written poems while working as a firespotter on a lookout tower in a forest. Poets, said Robert Frost, should either farm or else cheat their employers.

It seems essential that, like prophets who retreat to the wilderness, writers return to civilization to establish contact with the rest of humanity. That may be one reason we are all here. I can't believe that the stipends for this conference were enough to entice so many distinguished writers—no, some other need must have drawn them here. Working in solitude, writers feel an occasional yearning to connect with their peers. Clearly it is difficult to work in loneliness and to suffer rejection—to see the work of years flung back in your face with a printed slip or a snide remark. Every published writer here, I am sure, has known some lonely defeats. When Frost was an unknown, he sent a poem to *The Atlantic* which came back (he told the Bread Loaf Writers' Conference) folded and re-folded six or eight times, and with staples banged through it—perhaps an all-time record for the most emphatic rejection of a poem. So it helps to attend a writers' conference and take comfort in the fact that you aren't completely alone.

You connect with people profoundly, to be sure, when you write of lives other than your own. When Robert Olen Butler writes a story in the first person as a Vietnamese displaced to Louisiana, the process of his writing has clearly involved personal connections with Vietnamese-Americans and much conscientious reporting. The Irish poet George Moore, on the other hand, once edited an *Anthology of Pure Poetry*, in which most of the poems consisted of pleasing images and eschewed any kind of social comment. The book convinced me that the best poetry has to be impure and in some way concerned with the human race—not nec-essarily full of social message, but at least more interested in people than in rainbows and roses.

Some writers dread solitude. In a great poem, "Resolution and Inde-pendence," perhaps better known as "The Leech-gatherer," Words-worth voices his fear of that utter loneliness which can overtake a poet—of the miseries of the writer's life, of

> the fear that kills
> And hope that is unwilling to be fed;
> Cold, pain, and labor, and all fleshly ills
> And mighty poets in their misery dead.

As you recall, he is saved from these depressing thoughts by a chance meeting with a man on a lonely moor: a man crushed down by solitude, poverty, and age. The old man makes a bare living by gathering leeches, those bloodsuckers once in medical favor, yet in both speech and bearing he retains tremendous dignity. This lonely man will be Wordsworth's "help and stay." When gloom again impends, the poet will remember him.

One Leech-gatherer figure stands out in my own personal memory. He is James Hayford, the Vermont poet who died in 1993 after a lifetime spent far from the literary marketplace. Hayford lived most of his eighty years in Orleans, a town of four thousand near the Canadian border, working as a goat farmer, a music teacher, and a church organist. To the end of his days he seems to have kept a promise he had made early in life to Robert Frost. When Hayford was a senior at Amherst, Frost awarded him a prize of a thousand dollars—at the time, enough money to live on for a year—but with a few strings attached. The recipient was to avoid cities, colleges, and literary society. He was to keep to himself and merely write. Hayford did so, and kept on for the rest of his life. Unlike Frost, he was no self-promoter, and although a handful of his poems were printed in the *New Yorker* and other magazines, he was obliged to publish his small collections himself, and they were sold only in bookshops and gift shops in rural Vermont. Despite the publication late in his life of his collected poems by a commercial press, Hayford remained little known outside of his home state. Yet I believe him one of the finest metrical poets of our time. He has a wry poem about loneliness, "Latter Days." Let me share it with you.

> Persuaded that it will be lonely later
> When the lights are out and all the people gone,
> I who am always an impatient waiter
> Say, almost, let the loneliness come on:
> Let winter wind imprison me inside
> Where no fire warms the rattling passages,
> My future poor in hope, my past in pride,
> With no one present but the Presences;
>
> And let us try what loneliness entire
> Will do to a mind that sometimes chose itself
> Instead of company around a fire,
> Or found its company along a shelf—
> Let's see if I shall have the wit to bless
> Like early ills, this latter loneliness.

Like all good sonnets, Hayford's says something. If, like Wordsworth, you happen to find in solitude a touch of dread, then Hayford proposes a solution. Face loneliness—go into the wilderness. Loneliness is a disguised blessing. Bring it on, let it do its damnedest, be tried by it.

But Hayford knows that what he invites may prove terrible. He *almost* wishes for "loneliness entire." That qualifying "almost" strikes me as touchingly human—a last-minute chickening out. Solitude can be dangerous. Living in loneliness entire, a writer can fall prey to paranoiac delusion, and start thinking, "Some organized cartel or Mafia is dead set against me—that's why nobody will publish me!" In truth, the writer who thinks like that probably hasn't run up against the Mafia, but only met that fearful indifference we all meet—some of us, most of the time. Total solitude, for an extended time, can cause a writer to lose all sense of audience. That is what happened to a poet I know, who for the past twenty years has lived a hermit's existence. He pays me a visit every five years, and this year, it seemed that his work had evolved far beyond the point at which another human being might be expected to read it with any pleasure or satisfaction.

Platitudinous as it may be to claim, a writer needs not only solitude but also society. To connect with one's peers—even extreme loners such as Emily Dickinson and Gerard Manley Hopkins felt this urge. They wrote letters to conservative-minded poets—Thomas Wentworth Higginson, Robert Bridges—who came to appreciate their icon-shattering works only after the passage of decades. There comes a certain moment in your writing life when you feel a need to reach out, perhaps to be part of a group. If you lack confidence and don't quite trust the fruits of your solitude, a group can be reassuring. Some groups have attained fame—the Fugitives (Ransom, Tate, Jarrell, Laura Riding, Donald Davidson), the Beats. As a young graduate student in Ann Arbor, I had the good fortune to arrive in town along with some fellow aspiring poets—Keith Waldrop, James Camp, Dallas Wiebe, Donald Hope. Over beer, we'd trade scathing criticism of one another's poems, and sometimes the group would be joined by an established professional: Donald Hall or W. D. Snodgrass. That is the intrinsic value of a group. The scarcest and most vital experience a poet can have is to be read with close attention. So you exchange attention.

Such an exchange happens in an MFA writing workshop on a campus these days, a situation in which a group of peers is provided all ready-made. I used to think that such workshops formed and developed writers, but Jonathan Holden convinced me otherwise. Young writers, by banding together, form workshops. Writers, Holden argues in his book *The Fate of American Poetry,* are today like medieval monks, driven by the barbarity of the world into the refuge of MFA programs, their monasteries.

In fact, not only student writers but professional writers who teach find on a campus a nourishing kind of society. Saul Bellow, who still feels the need to teach (these days at Boston University), lately told an interviewer that teaching "solves the old problem: what does a writer do in the afternoon?" Teaching can be draining—as can any paying job—but in teaching, at least you're involved with people of similar mind. Teaching, it's true, can take all your time if you allow it to. Successful writer-teachers, I have found, give fair service in return for their wages, but don't give students the last ounce of their own blood.

In other quiet ways, a writer relates to society. Sending out what one writes is such a way, although some writers make the mistake of expecting an editor to provide all the sympathetic attention a writer calls for. Never to send anything out is to risk the dangerous, paranoiac kind of solitude. In a sense, even a rejection is a connection to the human race. You laid your work on the line and somebody dumped on it.

To juggle solitude and society is every writer's precarious balancing act. No one has written better about this problem than Philip Larkin. Although Larkin's posthumously printed letters and Andrew Motion's recent biography reveal the Hull poet's personal life to be just as unpleasant as some of his poems hint, his best poems seem miracles. In one of them, "Vers de Société," Larkin shows us the rock-bottom worst about both solitude and society. A party can be a meaningless waste of time: drinking rotgut sherry and trying to make conversation with people who haven't read anything but the British equivalent of *Consumer Reports.* At first, the poet wouldn't dream of accepting an invitation from social impresario Warlock-Williams to join a "crowd of craps"—better to stay home alone and observe the crescent moon "thinned to an air-sharpened blade." But "loneliness entire" (to quote James Hayford) renders him vulnerable to his own darkest thoughts. He can hardly be blamed for chickening out and embracing society, however miserable.

> Only the young can be alone freely.
> The time is shorter now for company,
> And sitting by a lamp more often brings
> Not peace, but other things.
> Beyond the light stand failure and remorse
> Whispering *Dear Warlock-Williams: Why, of course—*

Given a choice of more society or more solitude, I'd choose solitude every time. To attend every conference, to court literary acquaintance, to butter up critics and editors and grant-givers can indeed help you make a short-term noise in the world. If that's all you want, or if all you want is to make money, then go to it. But to stick around after you're dead—to lodge a few lines or a few pages in readers' memories, to make them stick so hard that they refuse to go away—then the best course may be to retire into solitude and try to write the best you know how.

A favorite image in the teachings of Zen Buddhism is that of the cloud. It drifts upon the wind, free and solitary, yet at the same time is involved with the earth that it rains on and from which it drinks the moisture that gives it life. I believe that writers, too, need to be cloudlike: individual, free, and yet happily involved with their surrounding and perpetually impinging world. There's a similar view of glad but connected solitude in a small but ample poem by Emily Dickinson that I've loved for a long time:

How happy is the little Stone
That rambles in the Road alone,
And doesn't care about Careers
And Exigencies never fears—
Whose Coat of elemental Brown
A passing Universe put on,
And independent as the Sun
Associates or glows alone,
Fulfilling absolute Decree
In casual simplicity—

Now, many writers feel they must dwell in some metropolis—New York or San Francisco, where the literary action is—like little stones rushing to be part of a pebble beach. I know some writers who live quite happily and productively in San Francisco or New York, but for others, I think, such a metropolis is a quicksand pit. When I was a kid I used to hang around the San Remo bar in Greenwich Village just to hear the would-be novelists and poets talk. They'd hold forth by the hour about the great magnum opera they planned to do. I've never heard that any of them ever printed a line. New York can be seductive that way. You can get to believe you're a writer without ever having to write. A well-known poet who lives in New

York told me that for him living in the city has one other disadvantage: he feels obliged to spend all his evenings going to all his friends' poetry readings. Such intense literary society always risks becoming counterproductive. Anyway, Emily Dickinson's poem suggests that you can be happy and connected even though you ramble the remote roads of West Virginia or Montana or rural Connecticut.

Wherever you are, there's always the mail—and now there's e-mail besides. Already you can electronically submit poems to certain magazines and receive nearly instantaneous acceptance or rejection. I prefer the old-fangled Postal Service, myself. It may lose things, but nobody yammers at you through a printer, demanding an instant response. When you mail off manuscripts it takes awhile to have them returned, and your hopes have time to recharge.

A writer who did a classic job of maintaining his balance, I think, is Thoreau. In his cabin, where he went to find solitude and "drive life into a corner," he was often visited by curious squirrels and friends and acquaintances. I think of him waving to the engineers and the firemen of passing trains, and (although *Walden* doesn't mention this) going home now and again to his mother's house in Concord for a square meal. Solitary he often was, more so in winter, and yet he maintained a firm connection both to the cosmos and to the world.

To be solitary but not lonely—that is the task every writer faces. If you and I succeed, then we will be alone but never entirely lonely: connected to self, to our readers, to our fellow writers, and to the rest of humankind.

MARVIN BELL

Straw, Feathers & Dust

[BREAD LOAF WRITERS' CONFERENCE]

Where writers gather, it can be almost frighteningly lively. I know enough of you personally to know how . . . unusual, individual, odd, eccentric, sometimes nearly extra-terrestrial writers can be. I think a part of the splendid anticipation we feel for gatherings such as this lies in the fact that many practical people don't quite "get" what we do or why we do it: it conflicts with their view of the world as rational, sensible, and civic. And many professors still don't quite believe that we can, in some sense, "teach" it: the artist's traditional trust in process and in a studio format troubles their sense of the primacy of the product as it has been propped up in the classroom.

For me, the special circumstance of the writer who teaches writers—certainly, my situation—was well expressed in one of the *Star Trek* movies. Some of you may know that James T. Kirk, captain of the original Starship Enterprise, is from Iowa. Actually, it is a bit more precise to say that he *will* be. Gene Roddenberry, the creator of *Star Trek*, noted in one of his books that Captain Kirk was born in Iowa. Consequently, in Riverside, Iowa, just up the road from where I live, there is today a gravestone bearing James T. Kirk's future birth date.

Well, my reference is to the movie *Star Trek IV: The Voyage Home*, in which Kirk and his crew have returned to San Francisco in 1986. For reasons I will leave out, they need to take away two humpback whales, and there comes a moment when Kirk must persuade the woman who oversees the whales at the aquarium to help him. He decides that he is simply going to have to fess up about who he really is and where he has come from. We see them eating pizza in a sort of singles bar. The camera wanders the noisy room, then homes in on Kirk and his companion when suddenly we hear her blurt out, "You mean you're from OUTER SPACE?" "No," says Kirk, "I'm from Iowa. I only *work* in outer space."

I wouldn't have it any other way. I know that each of you has come to Bread Loaf Mountain from your own planet and for personal reasons. And that the great variety of offerings on the schedule still represents but a tiny sampling of your interests and discrete identities. During the next ten days of Bread Loaf, you will fan out to take up particular aspects of reading and writing. But today, as the conference starts to pick up speed, as it edges toward the content and tone by which it will be known and described years hence, and while we are gathered in one room, each one of us wondering if the dance to occur later will include the music in his or her head—while we are together, I would like to say a little about what we have in common and who we are as a group. I mean to stand up today, not only for what we share but also for our differences, not only for our knowledge but also for our ignorance, not only for our experience but also for our future. When Picasso was asked which of his own paintings was his favorite, he is said to have replied, "The next one." I can't imagine it any other way.

So: like the members of a guild, we are the same and we are different, each from each and all of us together from the members of other guilds. The poet Jack Gilbert imagined the place of writing in society in a poem which he titled, with his tongue in his cheek, "In Dispraise of Poetry":

> When the King of Siam disliked a courtier,
> He gave him a beautiful white elephant.
> The miracle beast deserved such ritual
> That to care for him properly meant ruin.
> Yet to care for him improperly was worse.
> It appears the gift could not be refused.

In other words, like an elephant in a country where such a beast is sacred, poetry—fiction and nonfiction, too—doesn't need a purpose to come into being.

For all the great sociopolitical issues we cannot escape as writers (and I'll say more about this later), it is still true that most young writers, having begun to write for whatever reason, continue because they can't help it. Sometimes it's just the materials that have taken hold of us for what then turns into a lifetime. One of us loves rhythm and sound, another loves stories and character, a third adores syntax, a fourth is passionate for imagery, and a fifth is mad for metaphor. Or maybe we just like the way it feels when we write. We all know many writers who rush to their desks to write so as not to have to do something else.

The story goes that one of George Balanchine's dancers asked him what the ballet they were rehearsing was about. In order to dance it, she said, she needed to know the story. But Balanchine wasn't one of those choreographers who thought ballets needed to tell a story, and he said, "It's not about *anything*; it's just steps." But the dancer said again that she simply had to know what the ballet was about, and Balanchine said, "OK, then, it's about *time*." And the dancer said, "What do you mean it's about time?" And Balanchine said, "It's about fifteen minutes long."

In the same way, my talk is "about" this and "about" that, and it is also about thirty-five minutes long—and of course I'm not going to dance it in a straight line. In fact, before I go any further, this being a writerly crowd, I have a little quiz for you. I found it in a newspaper where it was used as filler.

If you've already taken this test, you don't need to take it again.

It's multiple choice. The question is: Which president, during a dark period in his term, said, "What this country needs is a good poem"? You have four choices: Abraham Lincoln, Woodrow Wilson, Herbert Hoover, or Jimmy Carter.

Now I want to tell you a story about Osseo, Minnesota, and what it means to be a writer. It was in the '60s. I had been in the Army in 1964 and 1965, where one of my jobs had me reading classified documents about Vietnam. Intelligence was saying, "Get us out. We don't belong here, and we can't win." But the war was getting bigger, and by the time I was discharged, junior officers like me were being ordered to Vietnam on three days' notice.

I had already probably saved my life by winning a transfer from the infantry into the Adjutant General's Corps. The infantry wore macho gold-colored crossed rifles on its lapels. The Adjutant General's Corps, by contrast, wore a red, white, and blue shield of stars. There was even a poem that went along with it: "Twinkle twinkle, little shield, keep me from the battlefield." The colors of the A.G. Corps were red and dark blue, said to be symbolic of the typewriter ribbon, and our motto was, "Retreat, Hell! Backspace!"

But you can always tell when a war is getting worse because the call comes for more A.G. officers. You see, A.G. officers, among their other duties, serve as burial officers, so when *they* start going to the front in numbers, people are getting killed.

But now I was out of the Army. Barry Goldwater, the senator from Arizona, who the voters were convinced might use nuclear weapons, had been defeated for the presidency by Lyndon Johnson, whose second term prospects in turn would be fatally wounded by the war in Vietnam. That seemingly endless war just kept getting bloodier. We were, as the song said, "waist deep in the Big Muddy, and the Big Fool (said) to push on."

And so Robert Bly and David Ray formed Poets Against the Vietnam War, and many of us took part in readings against the whole Vietnam business. And one Saturday afternoon—we had gathered to read that night in Minneapolis—we went off in two cars to do a matinee at St. Cloud State College elsewhere in Minnesota. With me in one car were Karl Shapiro, Donald Justice, Bly, and Galway Kinnell. We were wearing coats and ties and, except for my mustache, none of us had whiskers. We had learned during civil rights demonstrations a decade earlier that it was better to look normal.

Partway to St. Cloud, we stopped in Osseo, Minnesota, to grab lunch. It was noon. We went into a bar where there were a number of very large men in large farm overalls having a very good time. We picked a booth, and I headed for the bathroom, which is where it happened.

I was standing at the urinal. Now, I'm always expecting someone to burst into the bar bathroom at such a moment—when I am standing at the urinal—to say, "Hurry up, please, it's time!" And indeed one of those very large men brushed past me, and then I heard him say from behind me, in a somewhat drunken voice, "What's that on your head?" I had pushed my sunglasses up, and I assumed he was being friendly so I said, "Those are my Batman glasses." And he said again, "What's that on your head?" and again I said, "Those are my Batman glasses." I didn't look around. I still thought he was being friendly. And he said, in a slightly more belligerent tone of voice, "What's that on your lip? Whaddya got that mustache on your lip for?" But I *still* assumed he was being friendly, and so, still without looking around, I said, "I don't know. My father had a mustache, maybe I'm trying to be like him."

And then *he* said—and here his voice got stronger—"Did you ride in here on a motorcycle?" I could tell I was being challenged and I said, "No, I rode in here in a station wagon." But it didn't work, and pretty soon, while I was zipping up in a hurry and turning to face him, he said, "You know what I think? I think you're a fucking Communist. You look like a Communist. You dress like a Communist. You act like a Communist. And if something's going to start, it would be better if it started right here." And he took a step toward me.

But I held up my hands, palms out like this, and I said, "I don't want to fight you. I *like* you." And he said, "You *talk* like a fucking Communist!"

Then he threw a roundhouse punch at me which, being a small target then, I was able to sidestep, and I exited the men's room with, like they say, dispatch. My new friend came lumbering after me but never caught up.

The story goes on from there, but the point had been made. Some people just don't like writers. They don't even have to know you're one of them. They can tell when one is around, the way a speeding driver can sense a highway patrol car just over the hill. They don't have to have actually seen a writer to know they don't like you. They've heard. My father, as a young immigrant from what we called *the* Ukraine, worked for a while in remote New England where nice people, knowing he was Jewish, actually asked if he would let them see his tail.

There will always be people who know one or two things about you and assume everything else. Have you ever noticed this in academia or elsewhere? Have you heard anyone rail against all formalism or all free verse, or take critical positions against men or women, against narrative or the lyric or language poetry, against Midwestern writers or Southern writers or West Coast or East Coast writers, against writers published by corporations or those published by independent presses, against those who make money or those who don't, against those who write politically or those who don't, against those who claim—true or not—to have grown up blue-collar or those who grew up lucky? Have you heard anyone pigeonhole the

'40s or '50s, the '60s or '70s, the '80s . . . the '90s? How about Abraham Lincoln, Woodrow Wilson, Herbert Hoover, Jimmy Carter? Do we as writers indulge these sorts of generalizations? Of course not. We writers know better, right? We remember our parents' saying, "Comparisons are odious." We never forget that pigeonholes are for pigeons. We describe rather than judge. Don't we? Don't we? Of course we do. Let me tell you another story.

It's still the '60s, or maybe the early '70s. The crowd that has shown up to hear Allen Ginsberg is far too large for the room. Hundreds of people can't even get inside the door. From the street, we pass the word forward that we are moving to a larger hall. Soon six or seven hundred people are following our little advance group across a greensward when a young man pushes forward to ask Ginsberg a question. "Whaddya think of Creeley's new book?" he asks. By his tone of voice, we can tell that he doesn't, himself, care for it. Another disappointed fan. But Ginsberg delivers a terrific response. Turning to the young man, he says, "Whatever Bob's doing, I'm *for* him."

It would be good if every writer, and especially every teacher, could remember to take that stand as much as possible. I suppose that we may sometimes forget to because we begin to assume that everyone knows how we feel at heart. While we are complaining about some literary flaw in the work of a contemporary, or worrying over who got invited to the party, maybe we still assume that everyone *knows* that, whatever Writer X and Writer Y are doing, of course we're "*for* them." But everyone doesn't know, and it's time we reminded one another. To distort a famous sentence in our political history: If we do not have our hangups together, we shall all have our hangups separately.

I believe that a writer learns best from work that is significantly different from his or her own. Some years ago a writers' organization invited me to be on a panel about literary influence. And so I asked a very, very bright and very, very shy poetry student what *he* thought about influence. And he said that he had learned over time that, whenever he *hated* a book of poetry, but didn't know why, a year later he would love that book.

Here's a quatrain by Antonio Machado, just four lines of poetry that bear on the willingness to go where few men and women have gone before:

> People possess four things
> that are no good at sea:
> anchor, rudder, oars
> and the fear of going down.

As one who grew up on the water, I can tell you how important an anchor, a rudder, a set of oars, and even a healthy fear of drowning can be. But no, says Machado, "People possess four things / that are no good at sea: / anchor, rudder, oars / and the fear of going down." The point is, why go to the same islands all the time? Why have the same thoughts all the time? Why not abandon oneself to the medium (in the case of Machado's poem, it's the sea; in the case of writing, it's language) and end up in places—to use a William Carlos Williams phrase from his seminal poem, "The Descent"—places "heretofore unrealized"?

I had an idea once for a project to encourage writers to read other writers more closely—particularly writers who wrote very differently from themselves. Please feel free, anyone, to steal this idea. It could be put into play anonymously. My idea was based on a kind of chain letter to be sent to writers. Whoever received one of these chain letters would put his or her name at the bottom of the list and then would write a fan letter to the writer at the top of the list. But there was to be one more requirement, and this is crucial: the fan letter had to be . . . *sincere*. The idea for such a letter came to me at a time when poetry was showing early signs of becoming Balkanized—you know, little cells of separate identities, each with its own army trying to take and hold Parnassus.

But there are countless approaches to that mystic, magical mountain—which itself is dwarfed by the surrounding peaks of illness and suffering, good works and enlightenment—and writers who teach (not teachers who write, now, but writers who teach) know that sometimes a student finds a new trail. The teaching of fiction and poetry writing requires a certain amount of ju-jitsu and Zen. We each have our values but the method must remain tentative, flexible, receptive. For some years, I have tried to keep in mind one principle and one rule as a teacher. The principle is that the goal of the teacher is to set the student free. The rule is that, whatever the assignment, Teacher has to do it too.

In most of the poetry workshops—depending on the makeup of the class—near the end of the term, we put our names into a hat (mine goes in, too) and draw. Then each of us writes a parody of the poet whose name we have drawn. The writer of the poem puts the other person's byline on it, and when we gather in class a week later to read the poems, the person being parodied—that is, the poet whose byline appears on the poem— that person has to tell the class how he or she came to write the poem. It's fun, but it's something more, too: if you're in this class, it's the one time during the semester when you can be absolutely certain someone is reading one of your poems closely.

The magazine *Epoch* once listed the fifty best poets in the country. That's what they called it, "The Fifty Best Poets in America." It was a long time ago. There were many fewer of us. Still *Epoch*'s "list of fifty" had to be set in alphabetical paragraphs, one for each letter of the alphabet, and it contained, not fifty names, but five hundred. And even then, readers wrote in to add overlooked poets, some of them pretty obvious.

So when your chain letter comes, maybe the poet whose name is at the top will be considered, a century later, one of the fifty best, and *there* will be your fan letter proving what a sagacious reader you were.

Herbert Hoover.

In the meantime, which is where most of us find ourselves, we have other things to do than the business of ranking writers or circling the wagons. As Pablo Neruda reminds us in a famous essay, it's an impure world. Writing comes from a life, not the other way around. And writing is a way of life, not a career. As a teacher I have come to believe that writers are simply people you cannot stop from writing. They are helpless not to write. They will write as they have to, inventing rationalizations and prescriptions afterwards if required to. Some will write to be read, and others will write to be reviewed. Some will write for now, and others will write for a distant tomorrow. Some will write for beauty and others for truth and some for both. Some will write for the solitude and some for the spotlight. This applies as much to content as to style. Except for the occasional "occasional," they will write about the bloody issues of the day only if inside themselves they feel they must, and if they don't, they won't. In writing, as in teaching, there is still no one way and no right way. Louis Zukofsky's way is not less valid than Elizabeth Bishop's, Emily's is no less rich than Walt's, James Merrill and June Jordan both have a calling. More than any other factor, it is a reader's quality of attention that defines a work of art. This is true for all time, all texts. There is no writer in this room, no writer hiding in Treman or The Barn, no writer so new to language that he or she has not already paid some dues. Some people believe that you can tell from a person's writing how he or she will dance. But I think it's the other way around: the dancing comes first.

Nonetheless, we can not blink back the fact that the old Chinese curse—"May you live in an interesting time"—has come down to us with a vengeance. A short time ago, I was wondering aloud about this while out walking with my wife, Dorothy. I asked her how I could speak to you about the thrill of reading and writing (and teaching) when the world was suffering so badly. Sure, I could easily speak only about the worldly content of our poems and stories, but I had to confess that I feel an uneasiness about any situation in which writers might appear even slightly to want to take credit for their politics. Naturally, we most trust those with nothing to gain. In other words, I could live in a world of literary anonymity forever.

That said, the question would not go away, as surely it never leaves any writer for good: how could I stand up for free writing and the process that finds it when, to take just one example, the Serbs were still "cleansing" Muslims and Croats, and when my own beloved country seemed to the world to be more interested in enlarging its commercial markets than in stopping this latest holocaust? How could I talk meters and caesurae, surrender and abandon, when the West and the United Nations refuse to stand up to vicious nationalisms? How could the literary imagination ever again look at nature? "Literature is news that STAYS news," Ezra Pound said, but today we are forced to live inside a surfeit of temporary information. When we try to exercise our ethical muscles, we find ourselves in the ever-thickening mud of a multimedia, postmodernist, increasingly theoretical, preposterous—and, some might say, preposthumous—world of tautological witness. Did you know that, at certain alleged institutions of learning, it is now possible to obtain a graduate degree in literature without ever having read a so-called "primary text"? I wonder about such an arrangement. I wonder, for example, what kind of teachers and students can stand it. I wonder if this essentially approach-based method will turn literature departments into education departments. And, farther afield, I wonder if some growing fundamentalism, bearing an absolutely primary text, is to be the next great empire.

I'd like to take a moment here to make a bow in the direction of writer and publisher Bill Henderson's Lead Pencil Club, whose members receive letterhead stationery to be written on only with a number 2 lead pencil and which aims to be, according to its motto, "a pothole along the information superhighway."

But here we be, some way down the road, and as usual we know too much. Our government's vacillating response to the genocide in Bosnia may be an example of the consequence of being glutted, and perhaps feeling satisfied, with information. From the beginning, there was plenty of information to little effect. There is a report that, when Elie Weisel visited the State Department to suggest intervention in Bosnia, he was told that the president could not intervene because, if he did, it would injure his presidency. And when Weisel said that we had a moral imperative to act, he was told that the administration had a higher moral imperative, and *that* was to maintain the liberal coalition that the current presidency represents.

It was a citizen of Sarajevo who said, "You owe us for 100,000 dead, but we don't expect to be paid." And that is correct: there is no payment that would suffice. Wallace Stevens's lovely definition of poetry—"the mind in the act of finding what will suffice"—echoes clangorously in the marketplace of Sarajevo. And in Somalia and the Sudan, for example, during the recent famines.

Nor did Neruda's biting poem about the United Fruit Company drive imperialism from Latin America. Among the poor or oppressed, among the sick or homeless, among the enslaved or imprisoned, what poetry, what stories? Do we who are merely witnesses know enough? Are empathy and intelligence sufficient?

Conversely, when the poems and stories of physical suffering are written from the inside, as occasionally they are, by those who have reports to make, but have no stake in becoming writers, then sometimes such writings naturally take on an absolute rightness of unpremeditated form. A subject has found them and made them writers, as one might say it did for Anna Akhmatova. The intensity of truly grueling subject matter has so fused form to content that the writing seems, at least in its own time, beyond judgment.

Well, I was talking about this dilemma to Dorothy as we walked. And eventually Dorothy simply reminded me, as I had forgotten for a moment in the hysteria of the dailies, that it is also necessary to feed the soul.

Now, when she said this, we had been walking and talking a while. Before she reminded me about my soul, I had asked Dorothy to help me remember something less ethereal—to put on another pair of slacks after we got home—so now I had two things to be reminded about, and I didn't want to take a chance on forgetting what I needed to recall, and so I said to her, "When we get home, help me remember two things: to put on my pants and to feed my soul."

Let me tell you about two young poets who have had to do both in harrowing circumstances. I am indebted to Christopher Merrill for his report on The War Congress of the Writers' Association of Bosnia-Herzegovina, held in Sarajevo in October, 1993, during the eighteenth month of the siege of that city. Before adjourning, because the diesel fuel for the generator was running low, the association took time to declare that "the writer exists to face evil." The congress itself, like every effort to maintain normalcy in Sarajevo during the siege, had been a way of facing evil. For all the savagery being inflicted on the people of Sarajevo, one could still sometimes find there dance and theatre, film showings, even country music . . . and, of course, poetry. In the midst of the war, the young Bosnian poet Goran Simić had written this poem, "The Apprentice," as translated by his wife, Amela Simić. It's about writing and about war and about writing *during* war:

> I have spent half of my life looking for a vocabulary of beauty
> which will exceed the strange love of stupid paper and a smart
>   pencil.
> I have acquired knowledge from shadows, I have learned from
>   monuments,
> I have associated with ghosts.
>   Now, when I spend more time
> at funerals than at my desk, I notice how the covers of my
>   books
> of fairy tales burn up quite appropriately while on the frozen
>   stove I try
> to warm up the tea for my sick child. And how beauty returns
>   to me

through the ruddy cheeks of my boy and the linden flower I
could have never
supposed to be more beautiful than a rose.

Even when a body must struggle merely to survive, something in us—
call it the soul, if you like—seeks a less tangible sustenance. That seeking is, I suppose, what we would like to believe most characterizes our
kind: humankind. Hence, in the midst of one more holocaust, a young
poet again articulates the beauty of simple health (nothing glamorous,
mind you) and of the ordinary (not the famous rose but the common linden flower). When fairy tales must go up in flames to provide the fire with
which to heat the tea, what is the result: first, physical nourishment, and
then a new poem. I myself think this is a pretty good use of literature: to
produce food for the body and then to produce more literature, just as
conversation makes for more conversation.

But of course it would have been understandable for this Bosnian poet
to feed, not his soul, but his rage or his fear or his guilt. Here is another
young Bosnian's war-torn poem, this one by Ferida Durakovic as translated by Mario Suško. Her poem is called "Paper Tea":

Not something to die of: to wait
for the night to descend, gathered within
like a family in a room.
Real people die of something else!
On the banks, in a field, in a jungle—
of water, of lightning, of a tiger.

And you—you'd like to drop down dead from the flash of a
tiger's blood in the darkness!
Nicely, and quietly, with no blood and no screaming.
Just like in books,
as on the wing of the Snow Queen.

But wait a bit. The summer night will descend,
on the city and things, and on us.
We'll drown sorrowfully by sleep.

You'll wake up like dust on your desk.
Yet the better ones will die of something else:

on the banks, in the field, in a jungle—
of water, of lightning, of a tiger . . .

Here is the unreality of war, the frightening anticipation of an unnatural death, and perhaps, heartbreakingly, the guilt of the survivor. The guilt of the survivor is closely related to the questions that trouble each of us at times about the value of our art.

But Wittgenstein said, "The limits of my language mean the limits of my world." And the poet William Stafford, in a brief poem from the book titled *Allegiances*, wrote this:

Note

straw, feathers, dust—
little things

but if they all go one way,
that's the way the wind goes.

So, too, with our least important words. We can follow them. If we ourselves have weight, specific gravity, what Lorca called *duende*, then the most personal matters may have worldwide implications. Here's a passage from a journal kept by a therapist named Kay Morgan. It's from a section about her mother and language, a section she calls "Blood Talk" and which consists of daily entries made over a four-week period:

FRIDAY
    I don't know how old any of us were. My mother's age was my mother's age—that is, too old to do anything else but be a mother. Too old to be loved by anyone else but me. That is what I thought.
    Two things I knew about my mother: she was the second most beautiful woman in Silverdale and she could really talk. Mostly she talked a talk called Blood Talk, a term she made up, a term based on her belief that blood was the source of everything important and she had names to prove it: blood food, blood looks, blood songs, blood people, blood roots, blood time, blood land, blood talk.
    Real talk comes from the inside, she'd say, *you'll know it when you hear it so use it when you mean it, otherwise don't. I've only known one person who spoke it pretty much all the time and he was a pain in the ass. Your teachers won't use it, the Lutheran minister won't use*

it, President Eisenhower doesn't use it, those Bible people tried and ended up sounding silly.
All I can say is, it matters, so watch out.

Of course, I would never have been in that bar in Osseo had I not been a writer, but then again I could have been a writer without ever setting foot in Osseo. I had to be a writer to get there, but I didn't have to go there just because I was a writer.

Again from Kay Morgan's journal about "Blood Talk":

WEDNESDAY

And my mother said this:

How would you like to go to bed as Eleanor Roosevelt and wake up as Mamie Eisenhower? What a joke. They say Eleanor's husband said, "I've had war and I've had Eleanor. Give me war." Ha. Ike is anything kind of Everybody's Darling, but nobody's claimed any anti-wife shit from him, not from him, an old bald man like God. Listen: Eleanor was not pretty. Talk and not-talk get important fast when you're not pretty. Men who write books, they're not pretty, are they? See? Mean your talk like blood. Quiet, that's blood too; it can be mean. I'd say you're not going to be the prettiest so you'd better get serious about this. And stay out of famous, you'll say words you'll swear you never heard.

It would be unfortunate if artists, who themselves are often set aside as being ill-informed or crazy or, in the case of poets, just too weird for words, were ever to favor appearances over substance, or the group to the exclusion of the individual, thereby setting gender against gender, race against race, those who do against those who don't, those who believe against those who do not. I wonder what that men's room brawler would have said if he had known that I had been an Army officer with a security clearance, and that I worked with the Continental Army Command, the Pentagon, the State Department, and various embassies. (And I wonder what my colleagues at the Pentagon would have thought if they had known I wrote poetry.)

As writers, we have a chance—I would say, a duty—to make distinctions, not the least of which is that between disloyalty and disagreement.

Still in the '60s, Poets Against the War in Vietnam formed up in Chicago to read on the campus of the University of Chicago. James Wright was there, Robert Creeley, George Starbuck, Paul Carroll, John Logan, Wendell Berry, again the two organizers of the group—David Ray and

Robert Bly—Galway Kinnell, the fiction writer John Shulze, and no doubt others whose names have escaped me.

I remember the reading, certainly. However, it has to be noted that, except for the obligatory cadre of FBI men snapping our pictures, we were preaching to the converted. It counted because we were a part of a growing movement throughout the country to convince the politicians to end the war. But the reading was still largely a Literary Event. And the part of it I remember even more clearly occurred afterwards in Paul Carroll's apartment on the North Side of Chicago.

Now, James Wright had a prodigious memory. He walked the house at night reciting sonnets by Shakespeare and Edna St. Vincent Millay. He knew World War I songs. He was shy, so when young poets gathered around him at a party, waiting for him to do something literary, he would throw out his arms and say, "By day a poor and humble butcher, by night a fabulous tap dancer." And he would begin to dance and maybe to sing. His favorite trick, on meeting another poet for the first time, was to recite one of the poet's poems. And Wright was a great fan of John Logan's work. And so it came to pass that night, in Paul Carroll's Chicago apartment, that James Wright gave a spontaneous recitation, completely from memory, for twenty minutes, of the poetry of John Logan—in front of Logan! Now *that's* a fan letter.

Herbert Hoover.

Because there is no one way and no right way to write, there is no one way and no right way to talk about writing, either. No one knows enough. Those who say they know—run from them, run from them. We are all, as William Stafford's poem would have it, "Traveling Through the Dark." We are all, as Adrienne Rich's poem would have it, "Diving into the Wreck." If there is solace, and sometimes enlightenment, it comes from the fact that we are talking as we go:

> As I sd to my
> friend, because I am
> always talking—John, I
>
> sd, which was not his
> name, the darkness sur-
> rounds us, what

                    can we do against
                    it, or else, shall we &
                    why not, buy a goddamn big car,

                    drive, he sd, for
                    christ's sake, look
                    out where yr going.

Many of you recognized that little poem of Robert Creeley's called "I Know a Man." It could easily stand for the writerly circumstance, aesthetically and politically. The darkness surrounds us. What can we do against it?—Drive, look out where yr going. Is a writer someone who is always talking? Is a writer a nervous Nellie, or nervous Bobby, obsessed to the point of not bothering to get his friend's name right? Are the answers to the great questions, "Drive" and "Look out where yr going"? Is that dance slowing in the mind of man that made him think the universe could hum?* What are years? What is our innocence, what is our guilt?† And what rough beast, its hour come round at last, slouches toward Bethlehem to be born?‡ Is the best advice you ever got to put on your pants and feed your soul? Well, yes.

Nor may we come to know each other so easily. "My life, my secret," wrote James Wright.

Now I just want to thank you for your hospitality and for this opportunity to represent you. I am just a boy from the country to whom writers and their writings have made an enormous difference. Along the way, there were people who set me free. Writers. Teachers. People like some of you. My hope for us today, therefore, is that during this conference we will meet, not just around our knowledge but around our not-knowing, not just around the skillful past but around the experimental future, not just in the spotlight but in the shadows, not just while the band is playing but in the lulls. For as writers we are, as much as any people on the planet, lonely in our intelligence but comforted by our peculiar willingness to talk in the dark. Through the clink of ice cubes and the squeaking of

*Theodore Roethke, "Four for Sir John Davies."

†Marianne Moore, "What Are Years?"

‡W. B. Yeats, "The Second Coming."

chairs, though we may at times cheer this aesthetic and boo that one, though we may sometimes be required to decide between good and better, and sometimes when pushed to push back, one thing remains true for true colleagues, and it can be said this way: Whatever you're doing, I'm *for* it.

JOHN DANIEL

A Word in Favor of Rootlessness

I am one of the converted when it comes to the cultural and economic necessity of finding place. Our rootlessness, our inability or refusal to accept the discipline of living as responsive and responsible members of neighborhoods, communities, landscapes, and ecosystems, is one of our most serious and widespread diseases. The history of our country, and especially of the American West, is in great part a record of damage done by generations of boomers, both individual and corporate, who have wrested from the land all that a place could give and continually moved on to take from another place. Boomers like Wallace Stegner's father, who, as we see him in *The Big Rock Candy Mountain*, "wanted to make a killing and end up on Easy Street." Like so many Americans, he was obsessed by the fruit of Tantalus: "Why remain in one dull plot of Earth when Heaven was reachable, was touchable, was just over there?"

We don't stand much chance of perpetuating ourselves as a culture, or of restoring and sustaining the health of our land, unless we can outgrow our boomer adolescence and mature into stickers, or nesters—human beings willing to take on the responsibilities of living in communities rooted in place, conserving nature as we conserve ourselves. And maybe, slowly, we are headed in that direction. The joys and virtues of place are celebrated in a growing body of literature and discussed in conferences across the country. Bioregionalism, small-scale organic farming, urban food coops, and other manifestations of placedness seem to be burgeoning, or at least coming along.

That is all to the good. But as we all settle into our home places and local communities and bioregional niches, as we become the responsible economic and ecologic citizens we ought to be, I worry a little. I worry, for one thing, that we might become so pervasively settled in place that no unsettled places will remain. But I worry about us settlers, too. I feel at least a tinge of concern that we might allow our shared beliefs and practices to harden into orthodoxy, and I fret that the bath water of irresponsibility we are ready to toss out the door might contain a lively baby or two. These fears may turn out to be groundless, like most of my insomniac broodings. But they are on my mind, so indulge me, if you will, as I address some of the less salutary aspects of living in place and some of the joys and perhaps necessary virtues of rootlessness.

No power of place is more elemental or influential than climate, and I feel compelled to report that we who live in the wet regions of the Northwest suffer immensely from our climate. Melville's Ishmael experienced a damp, drizzly November in his soul, but only now and again. For us it is eternally so—or at least it feels like eternity. From October till June we slouch in our mossy-roofed houses listening to the incessant patter of rain, dark thoughts slowly forming themselves in the dull cloud chambers of our minds. It's been days, weeks, *years*, we believe, since a neighbor knocked or a letter arrived from friend or agent or editor. Those who live where sun and breezes play, engaged in their smiling businesses, have long forgotten us, if they ever cared for us at all. Rain drips from the eaves like poison into our souls. We sit. We sleep. We check the mail.

What but climate could it be that so rots the fiber of the Northwestern psyche? Or if not climate itself, then an epiphenomenon of climate—perhaps the spores of an undiscovered fungus floating around from all those decadent forests we environmentalists are so bent on preserving. We try to improve ourselves. We join support groups and twelve-step programs, we drink gallons of cappucino and café latte, we bathe our pallid bodies in the radiance of full-spectrum light machines. These measures keep us from dissolving outright into the sodden air, and when spring arrives we bestir ourselves outdoors, blinking against the occasional cruel sun and the lurid displays of rhododendrons. By summer we have cured sufficiently to sally forth to the mountains and the coast, where we linger in sunglasses and try to pass for normal.

But it is place we're talking about. The powers of place. As I write this my thoughts are perhaps unduly influenced by the fact that my right ear has swollen to the size and complexion of a rutabaga. I was working behind the cabin this afternoon, cutting up madrone and Douglas fir slash with the chain saw, when I apparently stepped too close to a yellowjacket nest. I injured none of their tribe, to my knowledge, but one of them sorely injured me. Those good and industrious citizens take place pretty seriously. I started to get out the .22 and shoot every one of them, but thought better of it and drank a tumbler of bourbon instead.

And now, a bit later, a spectacle outside my window only confirms my bitter state of mind. The place in question is the hummingbird feeder, and the chief influence of that place is to inspire in hummingbirds a fiercely intense desire to impale one another on their needlelike beaks. Surely they're expending more energy blustering in their buzzy way than they possibly can be deriving from the feeder. This behavior is not simply a consequence of feeding Kool-Aid to already over-amped birds—they try to kill each other over natural flower patches too. Nor can it be explained as the typically mindless and violent behavior of the male gender in general. Both sexes are represented in the fray, and females predominate. It is simply a demonstration of over-identification with place. Humans do it too. Look at Yosemite Valley on the Fourth of July. Look at any empty parking space in San Francisco. Look at Jerusalem.

When human beings settle in a place for the long run, good things occur overall, but there are dangers. Stickers run the severe risk of becoming sticks in the mud. Consider my state of Oregon, which was settled by nester-farmers who had one epic move in them, across the Oregon Trail, and having found paradise resolved not to stir again until the millennium. The more volatile and scintillating sorts—writers, murderers, prostitutes, lawyers, and other riffraff—tended toward California or Seattle. And so it happens that Oregonians are a complacent and conformist populace, excessively concerned with standards of behavior, bland and pasty on the outside, spiteful and poisonous within. It is we who originated the present nationwide spate of legal attacks on gay and lesbian rights. And it is we who consistently rank among the top five states in annual citizen challenges to morally subversive library books, books such as *Huckleberry Finn*, *The Catcher in the Rye*, and *The Color Purple*.

This pernicious pressure toward conformity is strongest in those places where communities are strongest and people live closest to the land—in the small towns. When my girlfriend and I lived in Klamath Falls in the early 1970s, we were frequently accosted by Mrs. Grandquist, our neighbor across the street. She was pointedly eager to lend us a lawn mower, and when she offered it she had the unnerving habit of looking at my hair. Our phone was just inside the front door, and sometimes as we arrived home it would ring before we were entirely *through* the door. "You left your lights on," Mrs. Grandquist would say. Or, "You ought to shut your windows when you leave. We've got burglars, you know." Not in that block of Denver Avenue, we didn't. Mrs. Grandquist and other watchful citizens with time on their hands kept insurance rates down, but the pressure of all those eyes and inquiring minds was at times intensely uncomfortable. Small towns are hard places in which to be different. Those yellow jackets are wary, and they can sting.

Customs of land use can be as ossified and difficult to budge as social customs. The Amish, among other long-established rural communities, practice a good and responsible farming economy. But long-term association with a place no more *guarantees* good stewardship than a long-term marriage guarantees a loving and responsible relationship. As Aldo Leopold noted with pain, there are farmers who habitually abuse their land and cannot easily be induced to do otherwise. Thoreau saw the same thing in Concord—landspeople who in many ways must have known their places intimately, mistreated them continually. They whipped the dog every day because the dog was no good, and that's the way dogs had always been handled.

As for us of the green persuasions, we too are prone—perhaps more prone than most people—to orthodoxy and intolerance. It's not a good sign that we tend to lack a sense of humor about our values and work. We are too easily offended, a bit too holy in our beliefs. In Oregon, timber workers and Wise Use people are often more fun to be around than organizers and functionaries of the various green groups. Just compare bumper stickers. Ours say, "Stumps Don't Lie" or "Love Your Mother." Theirs say, "Earth First! (We'll Log the Other Planets Later)."

I don't mean to minimize the clear truth that ecological stupidity is epidemic in our land. I only mean to suggest that ecological correctness may not be the most helpful treatment. All of us, in any place or community or movement, tend to become insiders; we all need the stranger, the outsider, to shake up our perspective and keep us honest. Prominent among Edward Abbey's many virtues was his way of puncturing environmentalist pieties (and every other kind of piety). What's more, the outsider can see landscape with a certain clarity unavailable to the long-term resident.

It was as a relative newcomer to the Southwest that Abbey took the notes that would become his best book, in which he imagined the canyon country more deeply than anyone had imagined it before. His eyes were sharpened by the passion of his outsider's love. He couldn't have written *Desert Solitaire* if he had been raised in Moab or Bluff.

Unlike Thoreau, who was born to his place, or Wendell Berry, who returned to the place he was born to, Edward Abbey came to his place from afar and took hold. More of a lifelong wanderer was John Muir, who we chiefly identify with the Sierra Nevada but who explored and sojourned in and wrote of a multitude of places, from the Gulf of Mexico to the Gulf of Alaska. I think Muir needed continually to see new landscapes and life forms in order to keep his passionate mind ignited. Some people have to be in motion, and their motion is not necessarily a pathology. For Muir it was an essential joy, a devotion, a continuous discovery of place and self. Marriage to place is something our land and society need, but not all of us are the marrying kind. Some of us are more given to the exhilarated attention and ardent exploration of *wooing*—less given to extended fidelity and more to rapture. "Rapture" is related etymologically to "rape," but unlike the boomer, who ravages a place, the authentic wooer allows the place to ravish him.

Wooing often leads to marriage, of course, but not always. Is a life of wooing place after place less responsible than a life of settled marriage? It may be less *sustainable*, but the degree of its responsibility depends on the quality of the wooing. John Muir subjected himself utterly to the places he sought out. He walked from Wisconsin to the Gulf Coast, climbed a tree in a Sierra windstorm, survived a sub-zero night on the summit of Mount Shasta by scalding himself in a sulphurous volcanic vent. Nothing macho about it—he loved where he happened to be and refused to miss a lick of it. In his wandering, day to day and minute to minute, he was more placed than most of us will ever be, in a lifetime at home or a life on the move. Rootedness was not his genius and not his need.

Muir's devoted adventuring, of course, was something very different from the random restlessness of many in our culture today. Recently I sat through a dinner party during which the guests, most of them thirty-something, compared notes all evening about their travels through Asia. They were experts in border crossings, train transport, currency exchange, and even local art objects, but nothing I heard that evening indicated an influence of land or native peoples upon the traveler's soul. They were travel technicians. Many backpackers are the same, passing through wilderness places encapsulated in maps and objectives and high-tech gear. There *is* a pathology there, a serious one. It infects all of us to one degree or another. We have not yet arrived where we believe—and our color slides show—we have already been.

But if shifting around disconnected from land and community is our national disease, I would argue, perversely perhaps, or perhaps just homeopathically, that it is also an element of our national health. Hank Williams and others in our folk and country traditions stir something in many of us when they sing the delights of the open road, of rambling on the loose by foot or thumb or boxcar through the American countryside. Williams's "Ramblin' Man" believes that God intended him for a life of discovery beyond the horizon. Is this mere immaturity? Irresponsibility? An inability to relate to people or place? Maybe. But maybe also renewal, vitality, a growing of the soul. I know I'm never happier than when driving the highways and back roads of the West, pulling off somewhere, anywhere, to sleep in the truck and wake to a place I've never seen before. I can't defend the cost of that kind of travel in fossil fuel consumption and air befoulment—Williams's rambler at least took the fuel-efficient train—but I do know that it soothes and nurtures me as a man and a writer.

And if being rootless or even placeless is essential to some individuals, it may be essential in some way to the health of the culture. In Native American stories of the Northwest, I notice that Coyote doesn't seem to have a home. Either that, or he's sure on the road a lot. "Coyote was traveling upriver," the stories begin. "Coyote came over Neahkanie Mountain," "Coyote was going there . . ." The stories take place in the early time when the order of the world was still in flux. Coyote, the placeless one, helps people and animals find their places. You wouldn't want to base a code of ethics on his character, which is unreliable and frequently ignoble, but he is the agent who introduces human beings to their roles and responsibilities in life. Coyote is the necessary inseminator. (Sometimes literally.) He is the shifty and shiftless traveler who fertilizes the locally rooted bloomings of the world.

Maybe Coyote moves among us as the stranger, often odd or even disagreeable, who brings reports from far places. Maybe that stranger is one of the carriers of our wildness, one of the mutant genes that keep our evolution fresh and thriving. It's for that stranger, says Elie Weisel, that an extra place is set at the seder table. The voyager might arrive, the one who finds his home in the homes of others. He might tell a story, a story no one in the family is capable of telling, and children might hear that story and begin to imagine what they want their lives to be.

It could be Hank Williams who stops in, and he'll sing you a song (and maybe yours will be just the family he needs, and he won't have to die of whiskey and barbiturates in the back seat of a car). Or Huck Finn might be your stranger, on the run from civilization, dressed as a girl and telling stupendous lies. It could be Dean Moriarty, pausing on the road, and he never *will* stop talking. It might be Gerry Nanapush, the Chippewa power man Louise Erdrich has given us, escaped from jail still again to slip through the mists and snows with his old knowing. Or it might be Billy Parham or John Grady Cole, Cormac McCarthy's boy drifters— they'll want water for their horses, they'll be ready to eat, and if you're wise you'll feed them. They won't hardly talk themselves, but you may find yourself telling them the crucial story of your life.

Or yours may be the house where Odysseus calls, a still youngish man returning from war, passionate for his family and the flocks and vineyards of home. On the other hand, he could be an old man when he stands in your door. No one's quite sure what became of Odysseus. Homer tells us that he made it to Ithaca and set things in order, but the story leaves off there. Some say he resumed his settled life, living out his days as a placed and prosperous landsman. But others say that after all his adventures he couldn't live his old life again. Alfred, Lord Tennyson writes that he shipped out from Ithaca with his trusted crew. Maybe so, or maybe the poet got it only half right. Maybe Penelope, island bound for all those years, was stir crazy herself. Maybe they left the ranch to Telemachus and set out westward across the sea, two gray spirits yearning in desire.

> To follow knowledge like a sinking star,
> Beyond the utmost bound of human thought.

FRANCINE PROSE

Fiction in the Age of Caring

[BREAD LOAF WRITERS' CONFERENCE]

Writing a story or a novel requires finding one or more characters in whom the writer can stay interested for what may turn out to be months or years. That, says a friend, is why so many authors stick to autobiographical fiction. It's quieter and roomier when you are your only character, untroubled by competing voices, discordant human clamor. We hear that a character lives inside a writer's head or that an author seems to have gotten inside a character's head. But in fact the relation is less like that of homunculus to body or of brain parasite to brain tissue than like the close but often uneasy bond between family members.

One doesn't choose one's characters, exactly; one might not want to invite them to dinner or meet them in a dark alley. But there they are, fixtures in your life, and whether you like them or not, you keep hoping that they won't leave you, you keep wanting to know them better. Author and character are like partners in an arranged marriage; again, choice is not at issue, our characters may be less than wildly attractive. But with time comes familiarity and, ultimately, love.

Given this complex and passionate relationship between author and creation, a growing number of writers are more and more often perplexed to discover that through ignorance, coldheartedness, or just plain lack of skill, they have failed to make the reader care about their characters. Often, too late, they are surprised to discover that they were charged with (and failed at) the duty of creating a clear or at least flattering glass in which readers can see themselves.

I was dismayed to hear from a busy agent that many of the rejection letters her clients receive come from editors who have examined their hearts and found that, sadly, they just didn't care. And anyone who teaches a fiction workshop can barely get through a class without hearing complaints from students who didn't care about (or couldn't identify with) the characters in some unfortunate classmate's work.

One searches book reviews and journals for substantive discussions of content and form or for the most casual curiosity about a writer's intention. Instead one finds a kind of polygraph printout, charting the critic's quickening pulse in the presence of this or that character. A glance through a number of daily papers and Sunday book sections yields the following grim result: "One wishes she'd looked more deeply into these people so that we might not only laugh but care." "It's hard to really care about characters who often seem like parodies of familiar stereotypes." "But ideas do not make a novel. Characters do. And we need to care about them, deeply." Here, an author is praised for creating characters with whom we can identify; there, a reviewer claims to like a book because of its many likeable characters. (We may choose to think that this sort of critical discourse is confined to readers under the hairdryers swapping Gothic bodice rippers, but in fact it creeps regularly into respected literary journals and reviews of serious fiction.)

Of course, there's nothing wrong with caring about fictional characters. Some works make us empathize so painfully that we have to force ourselves to keep reading. Others achieve their effects by strong-arming us into identification. So "The Death of Ivan Ilyich" works its horrific magic by manipulating narrative distance, luring us from the safe courthouse steps (where the story begins) into the airless confines of Ivan Ilyich's sickroom until, when at last the dying man wonders if he has led his whole life wrong, the clammy chill we experience comes partly from imagining an occasion on which we might ask the same question. Nor is there anything wrong with being deeply moved by a character's fate. (It's often what we mean when we say we like a novel.) I remember how long it took me to get through the last hundred pages or so of Gabriel García Márquez's *Love in the Time of Cholera*, how I kept having to put aside the book because tears kept welling up in my eyes.

According to Mary McCarthy, length (that is, page length) and our involvement in the fate of the characters are two defining features of the novel, a definition that at first seems inclusive enough but then seems to suggest that Beckett's *Molloy*, Jane Bowles's *Two Serious Ladies*, Jarrell's *Pictures from an Institution*, and even *Ulysses* are not (whatever we or their authors might think) novels, since our interest in them is not about outcome, but about language, originality, the writer's quirkiness, brilliance, genius. (One can hardly imagine what it might cost the average book reviewer to care about Molloy, a weird creature no sane person would want to cozy up to.) And if the intensity of our "involvement in the characters' fate" is used as a standard, Stephen King is a better writer than Joyce.

It does put this talk of caring in perspective to realize how recently (the masochist can go back through several years of microfilm and find out) it became an acceptable response to literature; and one can't help noting how this literary-psycho-babble pops and vaporizes like a bubble against the wall of great writing. Dear Mr. Kafka, we read your story with pleasure but in the end found we couldn't care about this young man who turns into a cockroach. Dear Mr. Kawabata, we were intrigued by *Snow Country* but something about the novel (its chilly tone, perhaps) kept us from really caring. And "caring" is not quite the operative word in our view of Raskolnikov.

No one says they don't like *Moby Dick* because they don't care enough about Ishmael, that emotionally withholding guy who never tells us one word more about himself than he absolutely has to; nor that we don't know enough about Queequeg to care about him, either. (Of course we do care who wins, Ahab or Moby Dick, but as we read on in the novel and come to admire it more profoundly, we're less concerned about the approaching oceanic heavyweight match, and are in awe of the nervy genius of those chapters full of whale biological trivia, scientific data that don't come close to explaining the mystery of Moby Dick: ontological proof of God more interesting than Aquinas's.)

Who are our stand-ins in such novels? Jane Eyre? Isabel Archer? Heathcliff? Prince Myshkin? It's easier to see our own worst visions of ourselves reflected in Balzac and Stendhal's slimy social climbers, Flaubert's delusional provincials, any old fanatic from Dostoyevsky, a Jellybee, Podsnap, or Veneering. (It's probably more beneficial to see our bad qualities in fiction, instead of only our good points; but this way of reading may be ill-advised and even cruel in light of what we hear is a current epidemic of low self-esteem.)

Let's consider the question of how much we care about Count Vronsky, the man for whom Anna Karenina (as the song says) leaves her happy home. First we see him as Anna does; soon we see him more clearly: a handsome, shallow, charming man with an instinct for attracting female attention. (And it is an instinct, not a calculation.) In a brilliant scene, Vronsky's first meeting with Anna at the train station, an exceptional event occurs in the already charged atmosphere created when Anna and Vronsky first meet in the corridor of the train; there is a crackle of sexual static that Tolstoy registers beautifully. Anna has traveled with Vronsky's mother; her brother (there to meet her) knows Vronsky. Their conversation is interrupted by the news that a workman has been killed by a train. In an impulsive gesture that is, let's estimate, one-quarter sincere sympathy, one-quarter the high spirits and charity born of a new infatuation, and one-half the desire to *look* generous in front of Anna, Vronsky arranges that two hundred rubles be sent to the workman's family. We know what he's doing, and so does Anna, and we know she knows long before the moment when she recalls it and feels oddly guilty.

Already we are light-years beyond "caring" or "not caring."

Do we care about Vronsky? Surely our feelings for Anna are less, as they say, conflicted. And yet the truth is, we want her to go ahead and fall in love with Vronsky, ditch the stuffy big-eared husband. Hundreds of pages stretch before us, we want this love affair to happen! And we feel this though we already sense that it will be her doom, and besides, Vronsky isn't "worth it." That's how much we care about her—what kind of caring is that? Naturally, we don't want her to throw herself under a train, but Tolstoy writes those last scenes so strongly—so slyly—we feel that it can't be helped. (Much current book reviewing and book chat has a frankly therapeutic tone, offering free counseling to troubled fictional characters. Why can't Anna just get it together or join the appropriate support group: Suicidal adulteresses whose husbands won't give them custody because they're under the influence of French spiritualist quacks.)

But let's get back to Vronsky and to this question of caring. And to give him the benefit of the doubt, let's say: yes, we do care. Okay, he's not the deepest guy on the planet, but you could imagine being drawn to him, especially if you were married to Karenin. And then we get to the famous horse race scene in which Vronsky breaks his horse's back.

Vronsky, who is described as "calm and controlled" around horses, shifts his weight clumsily during the final jump and breaks his beloved mare Frou-Frou's spine. Not realizing what has happened, he pulls at the fallen horse and kicks her with his boot. Our feelings about animals are so much less mixed than our feelings about each other, and cruelty to animals is so much clearer a case. What reader could care about a sadist who could do what Vronsky does?

Well, this reader cares intensely, cares enough to go back and reread what has led up to this scene, how it was prepared for (Vronsky has been with Anna and arrives at the stable late, in an agitated condition), whose point of view it is written from, the heartbreaking descriptions of Frou Frou, and the meticulous, painstaking attention with which Tolstoy documents exactly what Vronsky experiences, what he sees, what he knows and doesn't know throughout the course of the whole race. We care about what's happening on the sidelines, where Anna is watching only Vronsky and Karenin is watching his wife watch only Vronsky. We care about what will change as a result of the horse's death and about the final prescient sentences that ring out at the end of the chapter like the tolling of a massive Russian church bell.

For the first time in his life he had experienced the bitterest misfortune—misfortune that was irremediable and that he was to blame for himself. Yashvin overtook him with his cap and led him home; half an hour later Vronsky was himself again. But for a long time the thought of this race remained in his heart as the bitterest and most agonizing memory of his life.

But the reader who has stopped caring—and who may by now have stopped caring about the whole novel because he or she can no longer care about a man who kicks his dying horse—well, that high-minded reader has another sort of caring in mind. For that reader, caring doesn't imply interest or empathy or being taken up by the vision or the brilliance of the writer; for that reader, whose ranks seem to be growing at an appalling rate, caring means approving of and liking (and by extension, seeing his or her own most honorable and attractive self in) a character, always in the most simplistic and reductive way.

That reader comes to us directly from the seventh-grade classroom where some overworked, despairing teacher dared hope that the boredom of rereading the same novel about a pioneer boy and his dog that was already assigned in the fourth, fifth, and sixth grades—that that boredom might be mediated by encouraging the student to have feelings about the characters. (Often, given the quality of the work studied in school, there's little that *can* be discussed besides the moral qualities—courage, independence, honesty, among others—of the characters.) In more nurturant, progressive classrooms students are encouraged to believe that their feelings about characters are more important than the work itself, an attitude not unlike that of deconstructionists who share this disregard for the text—though unhappily, without the feeling. The joke about the naive (preadolescent) reader who doesn't like a book because he or she doesn't "like" its characters grows less funny as that reader grows up to be the graduate writing student who tells me he or she doesn't like Kafka's "The Judgment" or Chekhov's "In the Ravine" because the characters are either "too" neurotic, half-wits, or greedy and evil.

Such readers could hardly be further from the "admirable reader" whom Vladimir Nabokov describes in the introduction to his *Lectures on Russian Literature*:

The admirable reader . . . does not belong to any specific nation or class. No director of conscience and no book club can manage his soul. His approach to a work of fiction is not governed by those juvenile emotions that make a mediocre reader identify himself with this or that character and "skip descriptions." The good, the admirable reader identifies himself not with the boy or the girl in the book but with the mind that conceived and composed that book. . . . The admirable reader is not concerned with general ideas: he is interested in the particular vision. He likes the novel not because it helps him to get along with the group (to use a diabolical progressive-school cliché); he likes the novel because he imbibes and understands every detail of the text, enjoys what the author meant to be enjoyed, beams inwardly and all over, is thrilled by the magic imageries of the master-forger, the fancy-forger, the conjuror, the artist. Indeed, of all the characters that a great artist creates, his readers are the best.

Now, two brief digressions—one pedagogical, one qualifying. First, I've found that children can often appreciate the very best writing and have more complicated responses than liking or not liking its characters. Not long ago I read García Márquez's "The Very Old Man with Enormous Wings" to my son. I read it quickly and he hung on every word, keeping up with the story. But when we got to the line "a Portuguese man who couldn't sleep because the noise of the stars disturbed him," he made me stop and read it again, and then he repeated it himself. In school he is as bored as I was with the same book I read then, a novel called *Johnny Tremaine*, though I did like certain gory or pitiful passages about the boy's hand, burned in a fire.

Second, the qualification: Ultimately, I think people should be able to read any way they please. Given the grim statistics (constantly being revised downward) about how little the average American reads, writers are grateful for readers, any readers at all. What's disturbing is the reader who is unaware of a way of reading beyond the literary equivalent of being the empress or emperor at a gladiatorial combat—Do we like this character? It's either thumbs up or thumbs down. And what are most worrisome are the proselytizing readers or the prescriptive critics, ignorant of a response to art that would enable them to read, say, Virginia Woolf, Calvino, Landolfi, Mavis Gallant, and countless other writers whose abilities to show or transform the world make the question of "liking" the characters irrelevant.

Readers brought up in the "characters we can care about" school of fiction will naturally want to encourage or, if need be, insist that writers create such characters. Logically, they may conclude that there are certain standards of caring that the writer should adhere to, a requirement that seems acutely unfair in an era in which kindness, compassion, even civility have everywhere reached a global low. Alongside the pecking order is the caring order: First we care about animals, then fictional characters, and, last of all, one another. Who are these saintly reviewers insisting that the writer care, the characters care, the reader care, when, in the world just beyond the book, we regretfully but routinely step over the homeless, and people are willing to torture and kill because of nationality and race?

What's problematic for the writer isn't injured vanity, feathers delicately ruffled by the shock of being thought "uncaring." The problem (the problem for us all) are these recessionary times, the fact that less fiction is being published. Magazines with long histories of printing short stories stopped doing so when their marketing departments pointed out that fiction doesn't "generate" advertising. (It's nice to imagine the advertising our favorite books might attract: Conrad's *The Heart of Darkness* bringing in large ads for luxury safari riverboat cruises, Kafka's "Metamorphosis" smaller ads for organic insect repellent.) The *true* masochist can compare the table of contents in the major Sunday books reviews with those from just five years ago; the number of novels reviewed and, presumably, published has diminished drastically. Every writer has friends with second or third novels they can't get published. First novels? Forget about it. In these down-market times, you can only invest in a winner, and the winners, we're hearing, are books with characters we can like, books that make us care.

It's a comfort to read Gogol, in *Dead Souls*, ranting against the same pressures:

> Happy is the writer who omits these dull and repulsive characters that disturb one by being so painfully real; who comes close to such that disclose the lofty virtue of man. . . . The delicious mist of the incense he burns dims human eyes; the miracle of his flattery masks all the sorrows of life and depicts only the goodness of man. . . . He is called a great universal poet, soaring high above all other geniuses of the world even as an eagle soars above other high flying creatures. The mere sound of his name sends a thrill through ardent young hearts; all eyes greet him with radiance and responsive tears. . . .
>
> But a different lot and another fate await the writer who has dared to evoke all such things that are constantly before one's eyes . . . the shocking morass of trifles that has tied up our lives, and the essence of cold, crumbling, humdrum characters with whom our earthly way, now bitter, now dull, fairly swarms. . . . Not for him will be the applause, no grateful tears will he see . . . not to him will a girl of sixteen come flying, her head all awhirl with heroic fervor. Not for him will be that sweet enchantment when a poet hears nothing but the harmonies he has engendered himself; and finally, he will not escape the judgment of his time, the judgment of hypocritical and unfeeling contemporaries who will accuse the creatures his mind has bred of being base and worthless, will allot a contemptible nook for him in the gallery of those authors who insult mankind, will ascribe to him the morals of his own characters, and will deny him everything, heart, soul, and the divine flame of talent.

Genius will always insist on itself; genius will always come through. But one can't help wondering (paranoically, let's hope) about our literary culture, if it could eventually inch down to the level of our so-called film culture, with its narrow ideas about cultural product. So that when the Machiavellian producer in Robert Altman's film, *The Player*, says that what a film needs to get made in Hollywood is, "Stars, laughs, violence, nudity, sex, and happy endings. Especially happy endings," one can't help fear that we will soon hear an editor's version of this. And what will we be given to read, what will our fiction look like if the forces of down-side economics combine with the forces of the upbeat and the uplifting—and the forces of delusion or (in the popular phrase) "denial" on a societal scale?

One: We will have lots of emotionally gripping, bittersweet novels about dysfunctional family life that are actually strident confirmations of the status quo. Most will be problem novels about bad things happening to good people—good people like us, nice characters who crawl up in our laps and affectionately lick our faces, confirming our most pious emotions and most flattering views of ourselves. The innocent victims of abuse, the deeply misunderstood—no wonder we can identify with them, their problems are just like ours! Most often the problem comes from outside the family—think of *Fatal Attraction*—though in more sophisticated novels the problem also comes from within.

So in a novel like Sue Miller's *The Good Mother* (a novel once compared to *Madame Bovary* by a caring reviewer) the snake in the Edenic mother-child garden is not only the possibly kinky boyfriend but the mother's own desire for the possibly kinky boyfriend, for which she is severely punished. Recently I reviewed a pop psychology book whose author began by saying that Anna Karenina and Emma Bovary were dead and gone, today's woman was no longer punished, not even for adultery. Not only did it seem to me that this author was living in a different world from mine—she must have been reading different novels. (Fictional women are still paying awful prices or being humiliated for sins that seem comic when committed by men.) Emma Bovary is a schemer, a fool; she doesn't care whom she hurts and in the famous scene in which she gives birth to a little girl, she turns her face to the wall. Sue Miller's heroine is sweet and sad, the eponymous good mother, who wants nothing more, really, than what is called a "good relationship." No wonder we can care about her—she's nice, like us, she loves her child, and she wants what we want. (When Flaubert said "Madame Bovary, c'est moi," he couldn't have meant that he wanted the world to see him that way.)

Of course there have always been novels about victims, outsiders, adolescents—Jane Eyre, Pip, David Copperfield—learning to make their way in the world. But they are rarely helpless innocents. (It's instructive to compare Brontë's prickly, enraged Jane Eyre or Dickens's Pip—a corner-cutting snob, betraying trusts, if necessary—with contemporary young heroes: boys who love their moms and are vulnerable and get so terribly hurt.)

Two: If the caring police have their way, we will also get lots of "big" novels without a trace of moral complexity, updated nineteenth-century boys' books in which the villains are villains and the heroes are heroes, though the heroes may (at least at the start) have the same problems we do or, more accurately, problems we'd *like* to have: substance abuse, infidelity, an excess of power and success that has led to spiritual or moral crises, which can only be resolved by an act of manly courage.

In theory, it's morally improving to care about fictional characters; it helps us learn to empathize with those unlike ourselves. But the good effects of this process are canceled out if the characters are so much like us that "caring" about them is simply a version of self-pity or self-regard. We have no trouble caring about ourselves, but we may still have difficulty acknowledging (and caring about) the writer, who may have a vision, a sensibility different from our own—one we may find uncongenial and thus not worth "caring about." (And yet it has always seemed to me to be one of the principal reasons for—and pleasures of—reading: to enter into the mind and see briefly through the observant eyes of a genius like Chekhov, for example, who was less concerned with caring than with recording the most minute and therefore most astonishing details of human behavior.)

If the politically correct ride their hobbyhorses to greater influence, we will certainly not be able to portray the world as it is, but must resign ourselves to describing a mirage that never existed—a world without victims, one in which writers cheerfully accept the limitations and forswear the "arrogance" (born of cultural blindness) of daring to imagine a character across gender or cultural boundaries.

Such writing defines the opposite of what might be called subversive, though masterpieces (even those by "conservatives" like Tolstoy) are profoundly revolutionary in their power to make us see things new. Of course, many writers (Calvino, Borges) have seemingly turned their back on this world and invented parallel worlds, though often what makes these new worlds interesting are their resemblances to our own. The danger is imaginative fiction that pretends to be realistic fiction—falsehoods from the right or the left about the most basic realities of the life around us.

Eventually, perhaps, a kind of segregation will ensue: characters we care about will be ghettoized into "caring" novels and excluded from broad, "uncaring," pseudo-Balzacian epics like *The Bonfire of the Vanities*, which I admired so much for its energy and scope and humor that I only rarely minded its show-offy meanness, its mistaking of misanthropy for even-handedness, its confusion between accuracy and easy know-ingness. I would sooner read Tom Wolfe than "caring" authors who reduce suffering to the level of whimsy. One thinks of the goofy grown-up kids who populate Bobbie Ann Mason's fiction, and of the kindness with which she spares them, or rescues them from, anything resembling adult grief. I would sooner read Celine (enraged, hate-filled, hateful) than writers who encourage us to applaud our own finer feelings, our high-minded, old-fashioned values, our faith in (and nostalgia for) the flag, Mom, and apple pie.

It's taken us years to learn that this menu of "caring" and gratifying self-affirmation is a diet we want to live on, though we have gotten plenty of help in educating and training our palates. For years we have been hearing that we are, at heart, sympathetic, good people, that we should cover our ears if anyone tells us differently, hide our eyes if anyone attempts to show us as we really are. For years we have been growing poorer, watching our schools and cities deteriorate while being told that our government cares, or, alternately, that caring is a euphemism for coddling and a waste of taxpayer money. For years we've heard that there *is* no problem, that everything is fine, that our trickiest social problems can be solved by the natural unstoppable outpouring of caring—by those twinkly guardian stars, those thousand points of light.

And why shouldn't our literature confirm a version of ourselves that we all can recognize and identify with? Why shouldn't our fiction unquestioningly reflect the fictions we've come to live by? We are an innocent, good-hearted, kind, gentle people—we're just having our little difficulties, our tiny misunderstandings, our brief run of bad luck. *What* difficulties? the caring reader may well ask. *What* tiny misunderstandings? How could something be wrong with a country—a world—so full of people who care?

SEÁN VIRGO

Raising the Dead

["WRITING THE LAND" CONFERENCE, EASTEND, SASKATCHEWAN, DELIVERED *EN PLEINE AIRE*]

This is a homecoming of sorts for me, to a marker and hearth upon a nomad's circuit, but three years ago I was a newcomer here, as I was a newcomer to Canada twenty-five years before and as, at the age of eleven—after a childhood in a part of Africa which is visually so like this Frenchman River Valley—I was a newcomer to the West of Ireland, in the village where my forebears had lived and died.

The landscape which surrounds us here is a most generous one, though it has blighted hopes, inflicted madness and despair, and cradled the extinctions of men and animals over the centuries. Its generosity consists of the gifts it offers when you go out into it—a walk through the coulees, a rest upon a hillside will always bring wild animals into your presence and as often as not will lift to your eyes something natural or man-made which has been lying for generations perhaps, in a spot you yourself may have walked over a hundred times, waiting for the moment in time, and the passage of light, that will introduce you to it. And if you bend and touch or hold it, you are at that moment touching a hand which dropped that object or cast it aside, fifty, a hundred, ten thousand years ago. You are annihilating time.

That hand-touch across time is the subject of this talk.

What I learned as a boy in Ireland, going down across the old townland where nine out of ten people had died in the famine of 1847, and where, when the last member of a family died, they simply pulled down the thatch upon her and let the ruined cabin be her grave, what I learned was a ritual. All children are ritualists, and if their culture does not provide formulae for them they invent their own. I formed the habit, whenever I stepped into one of the rectangles of stones which marked the sites of the old cabins, of murmuring "peace be with you all in here," and in that moment acknowledged the ghosts, protected myself from them and, as I only came to understand years later, gave their lonely vigil a touch of living warmth.

When I first climbed that hill behind us and came upon ring after ring of stones, overlooking this valley, the encampments of who knows what people or peoples, who knows how many years old, I had my boyhood ritual instinctively at hand. When I stepped into a ring, choosing what seemed to me the natural entrance gap, and spoke that little prayer, I gave and received a gift. And the dead, the spirits of place if you like, are a hundredfold more generous to us than we are to them.

All children, as I said, are ritualists; and I believe that all writers of value, whatever their sophistication or ambition, are—at the quick of their talent—children. It is certainly as a child that I am entitling myself to speak to you, in this place, today; with all of a child's subjectivity and —it's already evident—with unapologetic nakedness about what I believe in.

I was going to offer you a piece of recorded sound at this point, but technology and I are uneasy friends at best, and it did not work out. Perhaps an evocation by words will be more effective here, anyway. I ask you to imagine the sound of a trumpet or horn, ringing out and echoing off the hills, like the notes of the Last Post, if you like, fading down a valley at the end of a Hollywood movie, or like Tennyson's "Blow bugle, follow echoes, dying, dying, dying." The note is C, a tenth overtone, with a brilliant edge to it. It is the sound, recorded seventy years ago, of an English musician playing an instrument found in the tomb of Tutankhamen. The trumpet slept those thousands of years in the Valley of the Kings, and when that first note was sounded upon it, in our twentieth century, time was again annihilated, the English horn player was kissing back to life the lips of an Egyptian long gone to dust, was breathing for him again.

That is what happens when we touch those dead hands across time. It is what happens when, in the hills which Robert Louis Stevenson called the "home of the sleeping, vanquished peoples," we kneel and pick up an arrowhead. Some people, as most of you know, have the gift (an accurate phrase) of finding arrowheads or fossils, or birds' nests or rare flowers, while others, just as intelligent, sensitive, and moral, can walk the very same spot, repeatedly, and find nothing. It is called Serendipity, that quality, and I think that certain writers have the identical gift—to find what is there in a place, in a time, in a mood, and bring it to others' attention.

What we make of those gifts, or course, is infinitely various. Some people will see an arrowhead as a trophy. Others will call it a projectile point and classify it according to age, material, type, and finesse of execution. (That is the expert's way—and an expert blessed with imagination has the richest experience, without doubt, of his pregnant find.) People like me tend to move through a reverie of genealogy: from the sponge which created the flint—or the volcanic heave which spawned the obsidian—to its slow climb through the earth's skin, its vigil beneath the weathers, its discovery by man or woman, its shaping its use and its loss (whether in the hunt, or battle, or by accident). Often it will be lost and found more than once. The Lakota/Dakota/Sioux people, whom we think of as being ancestral on the plains but were in fact refugees and newcomers like ourselves, depended on Serendipity to find the arrowheads which littered the prairie, and use them again in the hunt. Who knows who they thought had left the arrowheads for them—unknown predecessors or spirits, alien and unnamed, but benefactors nevertheless. In Ireland we called arrowheads "elfbolts": those who came before us were both more and less than human—fairies, the good people, lost ancestors.

We all look to our ancestors, or if we do not, our spirit withers and goes dead. And as newcomers to the land—where a hundred years or a thousand years of settlement are in one sense equally miniscule—we tend to cling to what little we know, for the rest is mystery. We have our family heirlooms—furniture, art, and utensils—"things," in D. H. Lawrence's words, which "men have made and breathed soft life into," a grandmother's quilt, a grandfather's gun, the old house which great-grandfather built and which still gets used during seeding and harvest, even the shape of the land itself—the dugout a father delved, the fenceline or shelterbelt his brothers planted. But the things of today, mass-marketed tastes, leave us more and more cut off from our ghosts. And the rest, as I said, is mystery. We are an ill-equipped people to deal with mystery: our culture believes in explaining it away; people treat modern science—which is nine-

tenths reductive—with more credulity than the so-called Dark Ages ever
granted their priests.

I remember, just after I came to Eastend three years ago, that an old
gentleman, Ira Schmitt, passed away. Ira had been a good friend in the
short time I knew him—he gave me many gifts because, though he was a
farmer and a hard-headed man in his way, he held the tribe of writers in
great respect. There was a moment during his funeral service in the hall,
when I heard the people of this town speak as one, in grief and celebra-
tion: there was one ritual left to them which *could* deal with death and
passing, a ritual they had inherited, an ancestral voice. It was a poem, of
course, for what else could survive of value into this soulless time but a
poem? I have rarely been moved in my life as I was when the townspeo-
ple's voices, old, middle-aged, and even some young ones, took up the
words and music of "The Old Rugged Cross." That cross stands in a valley of the imagination, which could be in any land and time these two
thousand years, which asserts our place in the scheme of things, and
which does not turn in against Mystery.

The way to destroy a people is not to deprive them of their leaders,
their land, or even their language—the doom inflicted upon my ancestors—but to destroy or render contemptible those individuals—the
priests and the poets—who hold the memories and rituals of culture and
place in their minds and hearts, and can pass them on. My parents' nation
survived eight hundred years of occupation and persecution because the
poetry and song was not destroyed—it is that simple. Hasidic Jews tell
much the same story.

In the Aislings, the series of defiant beauty-visions which circulated
anonymously in Ireland between the sixteenth and nineteenth centuries,
the poet dreams of an unspoiled place in the woods, where a beautiful
woman appears to him and cries to him in her distress not to forget her.
That woman *is* Ireland—its land, its history, the bird songs and the language of the trees, held in the hearts of the living.

The Mystery, contained in the past which surrounds us and which we
neglect at our peril, is what concerns the writers I have respect for. It has
to do with where we belong, as much as with what we are.

When I spoke of the way I react to the weight of an arrowhead in the
palm of my hand, I was talking of the kind of speculation, or daydream,

which all undamaged children occupy silence with, a speculation which seeks to place them, through their imaginations, in the scheme (or chaos) of things, in the dizzying possibilities, threats, and promises of *scale*—the infinite and the minute—which may, typically, begin with that flyleaf entry in a school book: My name, Pottery Street, Eastend, Saskatchewan, Canada, North America, the Northern Hemisphere, the Earth, the Solar System, Space, more Space, the Universe!

Because to be an imaginative, fearful speculator in possibility (or possibilities) is what an unfettered child is, and what an unfettered writer is.

And to have an answer (or a journey) which deals in contradictions, in parallel realities, in both the scientific and the phantastic, is also the dual heritage of child and writer.

There is, for me, no contradiction between the theory of evolution and the idea of creating angels, between Pithecanthropus and Adam & Eve or, for that matter, Raven hatching Man & Woman out of the clamshell. But to be speaking in these near-abstractions is not my natural mode; I explore and express most of my notions in the dramatic forms of fiction. So permit me to flesh out what I have just said with two short sections from a story, "Waking in Eden."

[*The context: Two people, Slovakian immigrants, are waiting for each other. Helena, a philosopher's widow, is in prison. Her lover, Tadeusz, is a potter.*]

V

Helena hears rumors the world is the work of angels.

At night as the radiator shunts and groans and carries messages on its flaking skin. From other numbered cells along the hall they murmur and moan, cry out and curse in their dreams. Or laugh, sometimes, like children surprised.

She lies in the darkness, below the judas window, and envisions the ateliers of Time and Space like the galleried levels within which she floats, suspended. The children of light, labouring on our Creation.

Cartoons, maquettes.

Thumb prints upon clay.

Forges and kilns.

Baroque elaborations, roccoco extravagance, romantic departures.

She ponders the Mongoose, the Mamba, the Garfish, the Paradise Bird. She considers the Mantis, the multiple Tapeworm cyst, the Karoo moths which cluster together and describe a perfect flower.

The angelic craftsmen extending endlessly the symmetrical blueprint, the two-eyed halves-made-whole, decreed for the animals.

Her fingers count out, on her belly, the ranks of Legumes. The Peas which extend from the manifold vetches to the towering timber-stack of the Brazil Tree.

The fourteen possible lattices in the crystals of lava.

Leucippus' grains of matter.

Time and Space removed from *then* and *now*, from the linear.

Are there recruits, to the angels? Do our dead sometimes aspire to make new connections?

Within this Creation, she senses other ateliers, and studios. The minds of artists, or Anton's beloved philosophers, maybe. Receptive minds, pregnable, fertile. In one sense, female.

Is this where the Sons of God lay down with the Daughters of Men?

She perceives that the world is a work of art. That works of art are sometimes the work of angels.

She is not sure at all that she wants to go home. She is not sure, at least, if she really wants to leave.

She reaches down, under her bed, to her locker. Feels through her clothes for the jar which Tadeusz brought for her. Her fingertips touch the cool porcelain flesh. The unadorned, almost translucent gift has become her icon for the workshop, the divine marriage chamber that his inarticulate mind must be.

VI

The nature of porcelain is a human miracle.

Its discovery was an act and conjunction of Providence.

It is clay combined with the matter that turns into clay—the dissolute, weathered flesh of earth's oldest rocks.

Porcelain is the stages of earth's decay, combined and reversed, passed into water and fire, and transformed into permanent harmony.

It is translucent. It sings when it is struck.

The clay is *Kaolin*, the rotting Feldspar, *Petuntse*. It has been analysed, copied, perfectly (as a synthesizer "perfectly" copies Bach) reconstructed. But at some point in Time and Place, perhaps in the Hanyong Mountains, a potter discovered a saprolite pocket, where the clay and *petuntse* lay ready, combined.

The Chinese called it "White Jade"; the merchants of Europe tracked it down in laboratories.

At 2650 degrees fahrenheit, the *petuntse* vitrifies, while the *kaolin* holds the form which the potter created.

And of all the substances that a master-potter must learn, with all the provisos of accident, good and bad, porcelain is the most intractable.

It is the clay which does not forgive. Because it remembers.

It returns from the fire with every error and hesitation in its shaping exposed.

There are scientists who find a radiance in the infinite cells of Evolution which few of the faithful experience, facing Creation, who have come to believe that clay held the seeds of life. Clay had memory, therefore it recognised, therefore learnt, predicted, or guessed at least, therefore at length adapted. Life and intelligence came as one.

Adom, the red man, was formed out of clay, the dried alluvium of the Euphrates Valley.

Even the great workshops of the Orient used moulds for most of their porcelain.

Tadeusz throws the clay on his wheel.

Out of every twelve pots, he rejects eleven.

There are inherited wisdoms, acquired wisdoms, and instinctive wisdoms, and they contradict each other at every turn—but we can only make sense of things if we live with and cherish those contradictions: all writers must say Walt Whitman's words like a prayer: "Do I contradict myself? Very well then . . . I contradict myself . . . I am large . . . I contain multitudes." It is our job to contain multitudes, to be more than ourselves, and more than our times would try to restrict us to.

I have one acquired wisdom which came to me through a chain of three great writers: I am quoting a dead man who quotes a dead man quoting a dead man. John Berryman, Søren Kierkegaard, Johann Hamann. And Hamann describes two voices. The first says, "Write." The second replies, "Write for whom?" "For the dead whom you love" is the answer. "But will they hear me?" "Yes," says the first voice, "for they return as posterity."

"For the dead whom you love." They are the ones you would wish to be judged by and in the company of; they are the ones who watch over your shoulder as you write—and sometimes approve. They are also, quite often, the source of your inspiration.

Here is a ghost poem, or I think that is what it is—it is a poem about writing, I suppose, about the place where the best words come from (for they are gifts, too—dependent on Serendipity, not on desire). It's a poem that is very clear to me, and yet at the same time, uncomprehendable. Perhaps underlying it is the sense that the words are out there already, somewhere, in the spaces inhabited by our dead, in the natural world, waiting to be found.

REUNION

I who was dead
with eyes for everything
remember nothing.

I wake to the quailing lamp
to my shadow launched out
broken backed
to the ceiling.

Time swarms across my hands,
a page turned; papers skate
in the aftermath.

Called back from the dead
to that shape I was known by
I live in the echo.

Those hands lie, fitfully lit,
turned down on that desk;
this back waits rigidly.
Time shuffles round my chair.

The walls are a drape of shadows;
the rain-laden ivy vine
rasps in the shutters of my room,
I who was dead.

A door has broken in
at the back of the house;
Night swamps the passageway;
a coat falls in the kitchen.

You bring the rainstorm
inside these walls,
Junipers heaving under the steep clouds
and shingle crowding back down the strand
where the mountain falls

The walls come down,
wind upon rain;
the lamp through the wet trees
fawns at your brilliant eyes.

Half seen at the edge of light
a hand combs rain from your dark hair
Night weds itself to these walls;
Out from the shadows you come walking.

I am a chair, a book,
a knucklebone, I question
everything, I who was dead.

My cold face turns in the lamplight
at memory's edge.

Time has no answers.
You, who were living, speak.

But who are the Dead—apart from our immediate forebears and friends—who are the ancestors who clothe the land, who help us belong, if we listen?

They are not just human, certainly. If our ghosts can be intermediaries for us in understanding our place in the natural world—and I'm profoundly uninterested in my place in the unnatural world—then so too are the animals. It is so easy for us to grant animals that great contradictory blessing of short lives and immortality.

Thou wast not born for death, immortal Bird!
No hungry generations tread thee down;
The voice I hear this passing night was heard
In ancient days by emperor or clown.

No one takes issue with Keats about that—the nightingale's song *is* immortal; so is the cry of the coyote on these hills, the warning scream of the hawk, the catbird's monody.

All of us have affinities for particular animals—creatures we would like to be, that we respond to, whose attentions we should cultivate. The robber barons of Europe emblazoned their shields, banners, and tombs with the animal tokens of their pride, just as supposedly primitive peoples have their totems and exogamic taboos from the animal world. Animals are emblems for us because, I believe, they are intermediaries between us and the Mystery. The Dead, I also believe, inhabit that space. As I wrote in a long, meditative poem, years ago:

> I have this faith in the dead
> that they lie in the elements, that they are
> initiates and might be voices
> for the waking stones, the seething
> articulate fibres of wood, the grains
> of matter . . .

To get close to the Mystery, to be more whole, to keep faith with creation or evolution—call that vertiginous complex what you will—demands that we find those intermediaries. And in the shallow material culture of this time, there is a fierce need for writers to act in their turn as intermediaries.

Once or twice, at least, in everyone's lifetime, the offer is made—a chance for the interbreeding of spirits between man/woman and animal, and through that a gate to the mysterious elements. Permit me, once more, to flesh out my argument.

My first encounter with real cold—a laughably mild one from a Saskatchewan perspective—was in Newfoundland. At 28 degrees below, I found a weird presence one January morning, in my habitual walk along Topsail Mountain. The presence was silence. The waterfall which spills down the hill's north flank had been stilled. I stood in awe, because the laws of nature, as I understood them then, had been suspended. Sometime in the night a fox had taken the same path—its tracks skirted the silenced falls. Later that day I happened to ask a neighbor how on earth the animals survived such cold. "Well, I don't know, boy," he said, "I suppose they keeps moving."

RUNNERS

In the cold,
in the cold below cold,
unthinkable steel white zero,
they say that the animals
keep moving all night,
running, running against
the cold.

The fox ran out of the woods
and the river was not. His
cat track shows in the snow
that he stood where the white bridge
foxed his memory, that his four
paws dodged to one side
where the falls hung silent.

And he watched. What moved.

In the dry waste of the January
moon, the juniper stump
unravelled, sprang like a grey
harp open. Dead
ten years. And sang.

What had the fox seen,
quartering the hill all night?

Rabbits like white wraiths
loping under the trees, the weasel
a snake over snow,
the lynx on her great paws
restless, grey, and the foxes
running, running, against
the cold.

               The ceaseless feet
down the chill corridors
of the wood.

                    Suppose the fox
snapped at the white air,
running; he plucked by the ears
a rabbit, ran on,
breaking the bone through
the fur, blood dark
in the cold, eyes dark
and the stiffening, crystals
of blood stinging his tongue,
the rabbit in seconds a twist
of rawhide. Odourless.

          The white wraiths running
          transparent against the cold,
          the restless water struck
          dumb, the animals running,
          running.
                    This morning
I find an ice flower
cupped to the spouting stone;
there is life still under
the floe, though the waterfall
is humped into nothing but
ice and a snow bank.
                    Sun
shatters at my eyes from the swathe
between the trees. Alder cones,
juniper stump, the black
spruce—dark relief
for my eyes; then I see the tracks.

          The fox ran out of the woods
          and the river was not.
          He stopped where the river stopped,
          nosing the curtain of ice.

The tracks run into the ice cave.
I follow and peer out of the
white sun, into the ice.

There *is* a cave, there is
music, lightly, behind the
deathly organ pipes, a nudge
of black rock, a thistlehead
in a pure knob of glass
(seed yellow and silver leaf)
and the thick white curtain,
the creamy stalactites
under the snow.
        I breathe
as he breathed under the moon.
The fox ran out of the woods
from the breath mist under
the branches, where the animals
ran. I breathe on the mirror
for the fox face, dark
through the curtain.
        Slowly
the night chill touches my skin
through my clothing, my gloves;
I breathe out, on the glass;
he is waiting—
        The fox
      on his cat's feet
           running
his straight ways down the forest
of my veins, his dark eyes
deliberate,
         running,
running,
       against the cold.

The land around us is clothed by time, and time is the breath and consciousness of all the creatures, as well as our own small species, which

have passed through it. Somehow that sum of existences, in all of its misery, loneliness, and dashed hopes, as well as its joys and unfettered exultations in life, creates a loveliness, a coherent holiness that *is* accessible. Without it, life is a sleepwalker in a windowless room.

But I want to end with an attempt to see things from the other side, to see what we are when the land, the spirits of place, the ancestors look back at us. You cannot go into the land without having eyes upon you—we all know and sense this—and I would like for a moment to guess what those eyes see.

It is not so horrifying as we might expect. The land does not watch us with the analytical judgment of a human philosopher, nor with the informed rage of an ecologist. I will not waste time apologizing for the imaginative truth I am reaching for here. It does not matter if it seems to you merely one man's invention—so long as it moves you—any more than it matters whether Prospero's island is real, or Ariel, or Caliban, or that dream of Death into Life.

Not all the revelations the land holds in store are clear, or ecstatic. There are vaguely sensed moods and consciousnesses out there (closer to fairies, perhaps, than to specific ghosts, or animal cousins or the simmering web of *anima mundi*) which form, it seems to me, a troubled, lonely mirror of ourselves, at the edge of our vision, as if in a wind-ruffled pool. These too are the presences which shadow us round the house side or the barn at night, that race behind us down staircases—their place in the City usurped by "tarts and muggers," though they continue to prompt from the wings of our dreams.

If I choose to name these presences Trolls—ignoring the trend for cute plastic voodoo-poppets which America has gifted to the world—it's because Trolls both fascinate and move me: creatures described by Ibsen—in *The Master Builder* as well as *Per Gynt*—as being part of each one of us. There is fear and unease in acknowledging them.

But fear is a necessary part of paying attention to ourselves, and to the earth. This fear is not back-alley paranoia; it is not squalid but holy—it must be explored.

My father had a friend, a Norwegian, a resistance hero. He was glamorous to me because he had lost an ear and some fingers to frostbite, hiding out in the mountains during the Occupation. Once, when he was trying to tell me that courage without fear is not courage at all, I asked him what he had been afraid of, back then. "You see," he said, "I was terrified of the Trolls—they come looking for you."

Yes, the Trolls, in their eagerness to come close, do seem malignant. But they are clumsy, uncouth, and certainly too slow-witted to fool a smart human being, or even a smart Billy Goat Gruff. You could say much the same of some gentle, disadvantaged people.

The thing about Trolls, and the reason I invoke their name to describe the presences which watch us, is that they have no backs. You cannot see them from behind. You may know they are there, but only once or twice in a lifetime will they reveal themselves to you, and change your whole sense of nature.

In the wild eyes which look in on our campfires, the light of our hearths, our warm night windows, there is longing as much as fear, or hunger.

And in that sense of them yearning in to us, as much as in our yearning out to the dark beauty of the wilderness, lies the whisper of Eden.

DIBIDIL

His hands are so
cold, he comes
blundering down
to the rim of the soft land.

Under that thatch
the small dreams
settle around the hearth

There are caves in the
banked up coals
where walls dissolve

and birds flash
bright down the forest paths
while music carries
across the silent pools.

His fingers angle
in the sunlight
through the harsh
hillwater

The young fish
lightly
elude him.

He follows the water
to the edge of his world,
a shadow upon the
cliff top
staring

Poor Troll
he comes visiting
again in the moonlight

afraid of dogs, of
discovery, of
breaking things.

The cold light casts
his hand across the shutters
clumsy and fearful

The thatch is alive, it
stirs
like a shy animal's coat

Like a nest of mice
the small dreams
rouse and whimper

He shrinks like a
burnt child
stampeding back
through the night.

Poor Troll has
come visiting again
in the moonlight

He hugs the mountain
His hands are always cold.

On the Balance Between Art and Life: An Internal Dialogue

[WHITE RIVER WRITERS' WORKSHOP]

Dear Suzanne,

I can't believe you think it's a false dilemma. Yeats said it clearly enough for anybody. You have to choose: perfection of the art or perfection of the life. You can't have it both ways. Nobody can. Do you think you're special?

Dear Sue,

Don't you remember when I was little, six or seven maybe, and I walked out into the front yard and pronounced judgment on the neighborhood—a nice neighborhood, actually. Pretty white frame houses with neat square lawns, some of them with wide front porches I always thought of as grins. Kids roller-skating on the sidewalks with clamp-on skates, dogs behind picket fences—ours a Blue Terrier named Mike. Our house still enters my dreams—its gabled roof looming, then the dream camera moving inside to the stone fireplace, a thick white rug before the hearth, pale rose walls. Remember how the deep purple lilacs lined the back yard, the climbing-elms along the sides? But despite that scene, so idyllic, it could have been clipped from a '40s Hollywood movie. I looked around at the families living in those houses, at the mothers sweeping the front porches in their pastel housedresses, hair pinned up in rolls, and I wondered why they had chosen these lives. It seemed to me a strange thing—to grow through your own childhood, then marry and simply raise more children.

It didn't appear that those mothers had any purpose except reproducing themselves like gardens reseeding. I swore it wasn't for me.

Dear Suzanne,

Yes, you did. Later you even wrote a poem about it. Though if I recall the poem correctly, you didn't remember your intentions very well. Here's part of it:

> I remember standing on the sidewalk,
> hands raised to the sky,
> proclaiming I would not
> be married, have children,
> live in a neighborhood
> like this. But always
> we returned
> to the little house
> behind my real one,
> put on the long dresses
> with folds that wrapped us
> like gifts,
> the shiny high heels
> and the feathered hats.
> Then we practiced
> a dignified walk
> around and around the block.

Dear Sue,

You're right. I didn't remember very well. In my early married years, I think my only ambition was to have a handsome house and good furniture like my mother's. Though I had a kind of reverence for painting and literature and music, by the time I married I'd lost any idea that I might make art myself. I was appalled by and (I realize now) envious of my husband's cousin who, when we were young-marrieds in college together, switched—in his senior year—from chemistry to a degree in fine arts. Then he went to Madison, the U of Wisconsin, for an MFA. We—his friends and family—were scandalized. He grew a *beard*, painted a flag on his ceiling, scared us with his radical ideas.

Dear Suzanne,

You? He scared *you*? By growing a beard and changing? I thought you were the great rebel. Aren't you the one who got kicked out of classes in high school for challenging teachers on every possible occasion and disrupting lectures? Aren't you the one who made a teacher so mad he stood at the front of the classroom clenching and unclenching his fists? Weren't you some kind of early feminist, demanding equal sports for girls, and the right to take classes like "shop"? And you never even *liked* sports, had no interest in "industrial arts." You were a troublemaker in the pacific fifties, you loved causes and havoc. You were a red cape waving in front of any bull.

Dear Sue,

Well, yes, but that does go back to high school. Remember, I married young and had a baby right away, and while other people my age were out marching for Civil Rights and against the war, I was folding diapers between my college classes. I think of the '60s as having floated above me like a kite. When I finally looked up, I saw its tail slithering away into the blue. I was a conscientious young matron in those days, polishing my baby's white shoes two or three times a day, becoming the perfectionistic Scandinavian-style mother I seemed destined to be. When I graduated with a degree in English and psychology, I started teaching in high school.

Dear Suzanne,

So it was *life* you opted for, not art at all! And as I recall, when you finally decided, late, to get serious about your writing, it was your *life* that got tossed like old clothes to the Salvation Army. Your marriage did, certainly. Rather a '70s cliché, isn't it? Woman marries, has family, decides she has to "find herself," leaves husband, becomes artist. But cliché or not, it supports what I said in the first place: Yeats was right. You can't have it both ways.

Dear Sue,

It wasn't that simple. The marriage had begun to go bad *before* the writing started, as it happened. In fact, the writing was largely, at first, a *response* to the disintegration of the marriage. Then poetry became far more than therapy, it became my *raison d'être*. By then the marriage was in irreparable trouble. When it collapsed, I'd published a book of poems and knew firmly that poetry would be at the center of my life.

Dear Suzanne,

Do you mean you were giving up on men and the possibility of sharing your life with a man again?

Dear Sue,

No, I didn't say that. In fact, I thought I wanted to find another man, a soul-mate, right away. Another artist. Over the next several years I found quite a few "candidates," but only much later realized that I was always drawn, like a Southerner to snow, to men clearly not cut out to be life-partners. That may have been unconscious, but I now believe it was also exceedingly deliberate. Because I had come to believe, as you do now, that I couldn't have a fulfilling personal life and be an artist. In fact I think I lived out another romantic cliché—the artist as tortured "other," always involved in complicated, excruciating relationships. Much beating of breast and tearing of hair. In truth, there was even some consciousness involved. I knew the tension produced by difficult love relationships fueled my poems; I had to wonder whether there might be less destructive ways to produce that energy.

Dear Suzanne,

So now you think you have it all figured out?

Dear Sue,

Why are you so hostile? Don't you think there's any chance of balance? Does a serious artist have to give up everything else?

Dear Suzanne,

Most people who've been there—or who've studied the problem—seem to think so. Are you familiar with Howard Gardner's book *Creating Minds*?

It's a study of creativity based on the lives of Freud, Einstein, Picasso, Stravinsky, Eliot, Graham, and Gandhi. Gardner says that all seven figures he studied renounced the possibility of satisfying personal lives, and that such renunciation seems to have been necessary to the realization of their creative powers. He thinks all of them made some kind of Faustian bargain to ensure their gifts. That they were so caught up in their work, they sacrificed everything, especially a normal personal life.

Dear Sue,

What kinds of bargains?

Dear Suzanne,

In some cases—Freud, Eliot, and Gandhi, for instance—it involved the decision to live an ascetic life. In other cases, like Einstein's and Martha Graham's, it was a self-imposed isolation from other people. In Picasso's case, Gardner thinks there was an actual attempt to make a deal with God. If God would save Picasso's sister, Picasso would give up painting. When his sister died of diphtheria, Picasso apparently decided he had license to do anything at all in his professional and personal life, including exploiting others. For Stravinsky, it was an antagonistic, combative relationship with almost everybody he knew. Gardner says artists believe such bargains must be adhered to or the talent may be lost.

Let me quote a little of Gardner on this subject:

> I was quite surprised to find that the creators, in order to maintain their gifts, went through behaviors or practices of a fundamentally superstititous, irrational, or compulsive nature. Usually, as a means of being able to continue work, the creator sacrificed normal relationships in the personal sphere. The kind of bargain may vary, but the tenacity with which it is maintained seems consistent. These arrangements are typically not described as pacts with anyone, but at least to me, they resemble that kind of semimagical, semimystical arrangement that in the west we have come to associate with Dr. Faustus and Mephistopheles. Equally, they have a religious flavor, as if each creator had, so to speak, struck a deal with a personal god.

Dear Sue,

Do you think that's what Adrienne Rich was talking about in her Emily Dickinson essay, "Vesuvius At Home"?

Dear Suzanne,

Certainly. Rich believes that Dickinson "chose her seclusion, knowing she was exceptional and knowing what she needed." Rich is annoyed at all the biographical hunts for the man who, it's assumed, rejected Dickinson and caused her to choose poetry as a second-best preoccupation. Ted Hughes "misses the point," Rich tells us, seeing Dickinson's redirected energies going toward the religious through her poems, rather than toward art.

This is Hughes:

> The eruption of [Dickinson's] imagination and poetry followed when she shifted her passion, with the energy of desperation, from [the] lost man onto his only possible substitute—the universe in its Divine aspect. . . . Thereafter, the marriage that had been denied in the real world went forward in the spiritual . . . just as the Universe in its Divine aspect became the mirror image of her "husband," so the whole religious dilemma of New England, at that most critical moment in history, became the mirror image of her relationship to him, of her "marriage" in fact.

On the contrary, says Rich, Dickinson's rejection of marriage and family was probably an unconscious decision, but a decision nevertheless, that suited the central design of her life. She did *not* dedicate herself to religion. She dedicated herself to poetry. Yes, she nursed her mother through illness, she baked bread, gardened, tended to myriad domestic chores. But when she retreated to her own room with its small table and wide-paned windows, the breeze through her sheer white curtains was the only breath accompanying her. There was the freedom to be the artist she intended herself to be and became.

Gardner would say that was her Faustian bargain. She was willing to pay the penalty of often excruciating loneliness in exchange for great poems.

Helen Barolini makes a similar point in a recent essay in the *Virginia Quarterly Review*:

> Though some critics, unable perhaps to conceive of women following so strong a call to Art, have taken [from Dickinson's poem no. 1581] that "Flash of waylaying Light" for religious dedication, the evidence of Dickinson's own words and actions

belie it being anything less than intuition into her poetic gift and the courage to follow when Lightning struck.

What would have happened to Emily Dickinson if she *had* married and had children? Would she have found the time and the private space to write one thousand, seven hundred and seventy-five poems? Emily understood the choices, and she chose well. Would you have had her do anything else?

Dear Sue,

Of course we don't know what would have happened if she'd made other choices, if her life had gone another direction. But do you recall, in that same essay by Helen Barolini, her discussion of Margaret Fuller, one of Emily Dickinson's models? Unlike Dickinson, Margaret Fuller lived

> as an independent, wage-earning woman very much immersed in the survival realities of the work world and national revolution [in Italy]. For her it was not a question of choosing between marital love and the joy of a child, or following her talent in a professional career. She was a proud, passionate woman who wanted to live out her nature both ways without settling for a half-life. She wanted what men naturally have: the full life of both love *and* work.

And there are other examples. George Sand, for instance.

Dear Suzanne,

I said, one thousand, seven hundred and seventy-five poems. Many of them poems of genius. Are you listening?

Dear Sue,

O.K. O.K. But nothing is impossible. Look at another example of a highly productive writer some consider as great as Emily Dickinson, who also managed to have a fulfilling marriage. Carolyn Heilbrun, in *Writing a Woman's Life*, suggests that the marriage of Virginia and Leonard Woolf is a good prototype for artists and writers. Heilbrun says,

Despite all the criticism that Woolf scholars in America have leveled against Leonard, and the scorn that Woolf critics in England have leveled against them both for their social position and class, these two had a revolutionary marriage, which I would define simply as one in which both partners have work at the center of their lives and must find a delicate balance that can support both together and each individually.

It was a mutually nourishing relationship, both emotionally and artistically.

Dear Suzanne,

Are you actually using the example of a woman who committed suicide to show that one can balance serious writing and personal life? Is that the best you can do?

Dear Sue,

I say it in spite of the suicide, yes. Because, although she knew periods of severe depression and disorientation, Virginia Woolf had a remarkable career as a writer of genius, and her marriage to Leonard seems to have been successful for both of them. Her mental illness was not a result of those elements in her life coming into conflict; Leonard helped alleviate her distress, he didn't add to her burdens.

Dear Suzanne,

I'd say that leaves a vast area open for interpretation. But rather than argue about the Woolfs, let me bring up a related issue that supports Mr. Yeats and me. Though many of us have been denying it for years, there's new evidence that the old cliché about the fine line between creativity and madness is in fact remarkably accurate. A recent *New York Times* survey of current books on the subject showed a genuine relationship between manic-depression, or bi-polar disorder, and creativity. Natalie Angier, the reviewer, says that in study after study, the findings are the same: artists have particularly high rates of mood disorders, especially depression. The ones who have bi-polar disorder, or manic-depression, often spend their lives on a see-saw between euphoria and a despondency so great they sometimes can't get out of bed. She says that many of our most famous creative people have suffered from the worst kind of bi-polar disorder. Others have milder versions of the same syndrome, and some have serious depression without the manic phase.

Would you agree that a tendency toward, if not severe, manic-depression is something of a hindrance to a satisfying personal life? If one knows one has such a disability, wouldn't it be wise to throw one's energies into art, rather than even trying to create a normal personal life? In truth, most of the writers I know personally have one form or another of this malady, and to varying degrees their lives have been "complicated," to say the least, by its effects.

Dear Sue,

What if bookkeepers were studied, or computer programmers, or stockbrokers. Wouldn't a similar number of people have the same afflictions? What's to say that this is a disease particular to artists or that artists should radically alter their personal lives and commitments to accommodate it?

Dear Suzanne,

That's my point. It *is* more prevalent in writers and other artists. Dr. Kay Redfield, professor of psychiatry at Johns Hopkins University, in her book *Touched with Fire: Manic Depressive Illness*, says, "Many people think this whole area of research is very squishy, very puffy and unsubstantiated. They don't realize how solid and substantial the work really is. The findings are that among distinguished artists, the rates of depression are 10–30 times as prevalent as in the population at large."

Dear Sue,

Pretty impressive. But there's another view even of manic-depression, which you're not taking into account. Dr. Ruth Richards, a psychiatrist at McLean Hospital in Belmont, Massachusetts, and Harvard Medical School, says, "People who have experienced emotional extremes, who have been forced to confront a huge range of feelings and who have successfully coped with those adversities, could end up with a richer organization in memory, a richer palette to work with." She also proposes that the excessive energy of a manic-depressive episode may give rise to a volcano of ideas that the mind can then shape into something meaningful during the less frenetic, more skeptical moments of a depression or a bout of normality.

And Dr. Robert M. Post, chief of the biological psychiatry branch of the National Institute of Mental Health, believes that because manic-depressive people are always veering toward emotional extremes, their brains become more complexly connected and remain more consistently open to unusual connections than do the brains of other people. That intensified set of connections between neural pathways, in addition to a continuing openness to the new, may enhance the ability to make strikingly original combinations of ideas—the essence of metaphor.

Dear Suzanne,

Which side of this question are you on? I never suggested that bi-polar disorder might not have certain advantages for the *work*. It's the life I'm concerned about. How does an artist with this affliction (or to use a more positive term, if you prefer, this *attribute*) make a personal life that's satisfying, that involves closeness to other people?

Dear Sue,

Surely you know that drugs for treating various kinds of depression and manic-depression have become much more sophisticated in the past several years, so that people who feel slaves to their moods, or who think the creative price is too high, can now have considerable control over their mood swings or their depression.

Dear Suzanne,

OK, so which of the artists you know about have made successful accommodations of life and work? Let's get down to specifics here.

Dear Sue,

You've read Dannye Romine Powell's new collection of interviews with Southern writers, *Parting the Curtains*. Do you recall that a number of the writers she talked with discussed the ways they manage to balance life and work? Interestingly, this issue seems almost exclusively a concern of women. Men don't tend to mention it. I think you'd agree that this difference is not a coincidence. Surely many male writers and other male artists must worry about the time they spend or don't spend with their loved ones, and the quality of their relationships, but the issue seems much more in the forefront of women artists' consciousness.

Kaye Gibbons, a novelist, also deals with the issue of her bi-polar syndrome and its effect on her work and life. The plus side is what it does for the work. She says, "I have found that I write best in what is called hypomania, which is halfway between being normal and being full-blown manic." She takes anticonvulsants now used in the treatment of manic-depression, rather than lithium, which she says "flattened me out and made me feel a desire to join the Junior League."

Kaye Gibbons writes about mother-daughter relationships. "It occurs to me," she says, "that my daughters are being raised in a household with a violently manic-depressive woman, and I look at myself through their eyes." The narrator for her new book, she says,

> could be any one of my daughters when she's thirty-five years old. And it's quite an education to look at myself through my adult child. It has made me get out of bed and stop being depressed—like stopping a car on a dime—on days I didn't think I could move. That vision of myself through my child's eyes has put me in motion and has helped with the illness more than the 27 pills a day.

Dear Suzanne,

OK, maybe having a family is a boon to Kaye Gibbons. But the majority of women writers/artists probably come closer in their attitudes toward this issue to Rita Dove, who says in Janet Sternburg's *The Writer on Her Work*,

> What's insidious . . . is the guilt that emerges whenever I need to take a block of prime time for myself: Sit the child in front of two hours of videotaped Sesame Streets so that a poem can be written? Guilt. Accept my husband's offer to stay at home while he takes our daughter to Kiwanis Park? Guilt. Hire a babysitter so I can write at my office at the university (only on weekends; otherwise students will knock to say: "How lucky to catch you here!")—in other words, farm my baby out? Guilt.

Maxine Kumin says,

> There was no question in my mind then—we are speaking of the early fifties, re-
> member—which came first. I paid fealty to my chosen role as wife and mother. The
> muse had to shamble along subsisting on crumbs of time, for to work outside the
> home in the middle-class canon of behavior was to neglect your family.

Dear Sue,

But Kumin is talking about another generation. In *this* period, women are
balancing personal relationships, usually including children, with their
work, and the work is not necessarily taking a back seat. Would you say
that Rita Dove's work has suffered as a result of her marriage and mother-
hood? Surely not. And if you've met her daughter, you know that Rita has
also been an exemplary parent, as has her husband, Fred Viebahn, also a
writer. And there are too many examples to cite, though I'll mention a
few.

Josephine Humphreys decided, when her children were young, that
the children were number one. That she could spend generous amounts
of time with them *and* write a novel. To find time for both, she tells Dannye Powell, she had to give up many of her other loves: cooking, which
she now does rarely; bird-watching ("Bird-watching," she says, "could
become an obsession with me. I try not to get out in the woods too much
because it could take over."); lunch with friends; entertaining. She keeps
a messy house, she claims, and is embarrassed about it. But clearly she
thinks these sacrifices are worth the rewards of guarding her writing time
and having time for her family.

Diane Johnson doesn't even feel there's a conflict. She says,

> How I think about my work is indistinguishable from the way I think about my nee-
> dlepoint or cooking: here is the project I'm involved in. It is play. In this sense, all
> my life is spent in play—sewing or needlepoint, or picking flowers, or writing, or
> buying groceries. Being a housewife and mother, I have duties too, but I am apt to
> shirk duty or wander off in the middle of it, so I can't really claim to have sacrificed
> my writing to my housework, the way it seems to some women that they have done.

Gretel Ehrlich goes further in her insistence that life and work can be
nicely combined:

Sometimes when strangers ask what I do, I say I write, but around here, they think I said "ride." I do both, of course, because most ranchwork is done on horseback. Writing is thought of as being cerebral work, while ranching, which takes up a good deal of my time, is mostly physical. But I couldn't write if I didn't ride and I'd find fourteen-hour days in the saddle quite tedious if I didn't have writing to come home to. . . . This whole business of dividing body and mind is ludicrous. After all, the breath that starts the song of a poem, or the symphony of a novel—the same breath that lifts me into the saddle—starts in the body and at the same time, enlivens the mind.

Dear Suzanne,

You're shifting the subject again. Ehrlich isn't talking about what we've been discussing—the difficulty of giving time and emotional energy to people, as well as giving one's all to work.

Dear Sue,

It's you who's shifting the emphasis. We're talking about life and work, are we not? Does life for you mean *only* relationships, or does it include all the activities, physical, mental, spiritual, that take our energies and time? Is the issue, in your view, still either/or, or is some kind of compromise possible? Maxine Kumin, in the essay quoted earlier, says it better than I have. She begins by quoting Margaret Walker:

Margaret Walker . . . speaks for all of us, white and black, acclaimed and struggling, when she says, "What are the critical decisions I must make as a woman, as a writer? They are questions of compromise and of guilt."

Kumin continues:

I like to think that a little guilt makes the world go round, and that the ability to compromise deserves high marks, for it is a learned skill. The life inside my poems was worth whatever it took to get there: guilt and compromise, tenacity, an inner secrecy that hid behind the facade of suburban housewife, Girl Scout leader, swimming instructor, chauffeur, and straw boss.

Dear Suzanne,

Maybe it's a question of a little guilt or a lot of guilt. For me, it's a *lot* of guilt, guilt I've carried around for many years and still haven't got rid of. Recently I wrote a long poem I thought of as a Faust poem. I *consciously* thought of it as a Faust poem in a woman's voice and had been trying to write it for years. And yet unconsciously I managed, for quite some time, to deny the central issue of that poem and not to write its most crucial section. I persuaded myself that the poem was finished, when all the while I had skirted the heart of it. Finally, after the gentle urging of poet-friends who recognized the avoidance (the void?), I wrote that section, which was all about guilt—the guilt I feel about my divorce, which was terribly damaging to my child.

Dear Sue,

Maybe it's time to get past most of that guilt and to think about your life now. Is it *now* possible to create a better balance? What are your responsibilities *now* to other people? What is your attitude toward your work? *Should* you live with a certain amount of guilt, as Kumin suggests?

Dear Suzanne,

In truth, my attitude is that I do not want to compromise. I still want everything, and I resent the necessity of compromise. My work is as important to me as any artist's is to herself. And there are people in my life— my son (at a distance—he now lives in Santa Fe), my husband (also a writer), my stepdaughter (who lives with us), and friends. I value those relationships profoundly. They take time and energy. But I want them and I *will* maintain the quality of them.

I'd like to learn from Josephine Humphreys, who seems to have found a practical solution: cut out everything extraneous to family and work. But I think I'm not willing to do it. I teach. I like to entertain, to cook and bake, to see friends. Recently I stopped baking bread as a time-saving measure. But I miss it too much and know I'll go back to it soon. My hands need the feel of that dough becoming elastic, a bit the way a poem does after enough kneading.

Dear Sue,

You're asking too much. You're old enough to know better.

Dear Suzanne,

No, I think maybe I really *am* figuring it out. You're right about the guilt, though. Not only is it time to get past it, but I think maybe a portion of it has been exaggerated or misplaced. Yes, my son suffered because of my divorce and my lack of maturity afterward. But it's coming clearer to me that my first marriage would almost surely have ended even if I'd never written a poem. My son was just as hurt as if poetry had been the reason for the breakup of the marriage, but the realization that it wasn't is at least partially freeing. And I am doing a better and a happier job now. My step-daughter is in most ways a blessing to my life, and I'm as good a parent to her as I wish I'd been capable of being for my son twenty years ago. I do most of the things that are important to me: lying in bed late with my husband on weekend mornings, reading, teaching, entertaining, lunching with friends. And I'm a productive writer. I'm not sure I could give much more time to my writing than I do, even if I had fewer activities, because when I'm in the white heat of the creative moment, I take the time I need to exhaust the impulse. Sometimes that's in the middle of the night. Sometimes I don't get enough sleep. But the poems get written, and *most* of the other things I care about get done too.

For the past several years, health problems have drained off some of my energy and I've often felt there were more demands on my time and resources than I could fulfill. But those problems are now corrected, and I can feel my old abundant energy returning. The surprise—to me—as this dialogue winds down, is that I don't think I have to compromise very much. True, I can't spend twelve hours a day working on poems. But I don't think my process would allow for that in any case. I'm a middle-of-the-night and morning writer. If I can have the mornings, most other activities, I think, can be fit into the rest of the day. Sure, I'd like more time to read, to learn tennis, to sit in on classes I've always wanted to take. But those are the desires of nonwriters, nonartists, as well. Nobody, I'd guess, has time and energy for everything there is to do in a life. But I've come to the conclusion that one can be a serious, committed artist and have more. A great deal more.

Even Yeats admits to having found happiness in his life and perfection in his art, though neither achievement led to complete satisfaction. Surely it must be the human condition to ask, even in fulfillment, "What Then?"

His chosen comrades thought at school
He must grow a famous man;
He thought the same and lived by rule,
All his twenties crammed with toil;
"What then?" sang Plato's ghost. "What then?"

Everything he wrote was read,
After certain years he won
Sufficient money for his need,
Friends that have been friends indeed;
"What then?" sang Plato's ghost. "What then?"

All his happier dreams came true—
A small old house, wife, daughter, son,
Grounds where plum and cabbage grew,
Poets and wits around him drew;
"What then?" sang Plato's ghost. "What then?"

"The work is done," grown old he thought,
"According to my boyish plan;
Let the fools rage, I swerved in naught,
Something to perfection brought";
But louder sang that ghost, "What then?"

ABOUT THE AUTHORS

PAUL ALLEN is founding director of the creative writing program at the College of Charleston in Charleston, South Carolina, and director of the Charleston Writers' Conference. He has received the John William Andrews Narrative Poetry Prize (*Poet Lore*) and a Rainmaker Award (*Zone 3*) and has published poems in the *North American Review*, *Iowa Review*, *Ontario Review*, *Laurel Review*, *Chariton Review*, and many others.

MARVIN BELL is widely known as a poet and teacher. His many books include *Residue of Song* (1974), *Stars Which See, Stars Which Do Not See* (1977), *These Green-Going-to-Yellow* (1981), and *Drawn by Stones, by Earth, by Things That Have Been in the Fire* (1984), all from Atheneum. *The Book of the Dead Man* (Copper Canyon, 1994) and *A Marvin Bell Reader* (Middlebury/University Press of New England, 1994) are his most recent publications. He has taught for many years in the University of Iowa Writing Program.

KURT BROWN is founding director of the Aspen Writers' Conference, and founding director of Writers' Conferences & Festivals (a national association of directors). He is the editor of the Writers on Life & Craft series, which includes *The True Subject* (Graywolf Press, 1993) and *Writing It Down for James* (Beacon Press, 1995) as well as the current volume. He is also the editor of *Drive, They Said: Poems About Americans and Their Cars* (Milkweed Editions, 1994) and co-editor of *Stepping Out: Poems about Hotels, Motels, Restaurants & Bars* (Milkweed Editions, 1996).

SHARON BRYAN is the author of three collections of poetry: *Salt Air* (1983) and *Objects of Affection* (1987), both from Wesleyan University Press; and *Flying Blind* from Sarabande Books (1996). She is the editor of *Where We Stand: Women Poets on Literary Tradition* (W. W. Norton, 1993). The winner of many awards and prizes for her work, she was recently a visiting writer at Dartmouth College and the University of Houston.

JOHN DANIEL received a Wallace Stegner Fellowship in Poetry from Stanford University and later taught there as a lecturer in creative writing and composition. He is poetry editor of *Wilderness* magazine and the author of two books of poems: *Common Ground* (Confluence Press, 1988) and *All Things Touched by Wind* (Salmon Run Press, 1994). A collection of his essays on nature, imagination, and the American West, *The Trail Home* (Pantheon Books, 1993), won the 1993 Oregon Book Award in Creative Nonfiction.

MARTÍN ESPADA is the author of five poetry collections, most recently *City of Coughing and Dead Radiators* (W. W. Norton, 1993) and *Imagine the Angels of Bread* (W. W. Norton, 1996). He is also the editor of *Poetry Like Bread: Poets of the Political Imagination* from Curbstone Press. His awards include two NEA Fellowships, the PEN/Revson Fellowship, and the Paterson Poetry Prize. He teaches in the English Department at the University of Massachusetts, Amherst.

JANE HIRSHFIELD is the author of several books of poems, including *Alaya*, Quarterly Review of Literature Poetry Series (1982), *Of Gravity and Angels*, Wesleyan University Press (1986), and *The October Palace*, HarperCollins (1994). The winner of many awards for her writing, she is co-translator of a book of Japanese poetry, *The Ink Dark Moon*, Vintage Classics series, Random House (1990), and editor of *Women in Praise of the Sacred: 43 Centuries of Spiritual Poetry by Women*, HarperCollins (1995). She lives in Mill Valley, California.

X.J. KENNEDY has published six collections of verse, beginning with *Nude Descending a Staircase* (Doubleday, 1961, reprinted by Carnegie-Mellon, 1994), to his most recent book, *Dark Horses* (Johns Hopkins Press, 1993). He is also the author of a dozen books of verse and fiction for children and many textbooks, including *An Introduction to Poetry, Eighth Edition* (with Dana Gioia, HarperCollins, 1994). The winner of many awards and prizes for his work, he has taught at the universities of Michigan, North Carolina (Greensboro), California (Irvine) and at Leeds, Wellesley, and Tufts.

SUSAN LUDVIGSON has published seven books of poetry, including *The Beautiful Noon of No Shadow* (Louisiana State University Press, 1987), *To Find the Gold* (Louisiana State University Press, 1990), and most recently *Everything Winged Must Be Dreaming* (Louisiana State University Press, 1993). A professor of English and Poet-in-Residence at Winthrop University, she is the recipient of many fellowships and awards for her writing. She has served as an editor and judge for the Associated Writing Program INTRO Awards, and represented the United States at the First International Women Writers' Congress in Paris.

FRANCINE PROSE is the author of seven highly acclaimed novels, including *Household Saints* (G.K. Hall, 1986), *Bigfoot Dreams* (Pantheon Books, 1986), *Primitive People* (Farrar, Straus & Giroux, 1992), *The Peacable Kingdom* (Farrar, Straus & Giroux, 1993), and *Hunters and Gatherers* (Farrar, Straus & Giroux, 1995). She is also the author of a volume of short stories, *Women and Children First* (Ivy Books, 1989). For many years, she has been a member of the faculty at Bread Loaf Writers' Conference.

ROBERT MICHAEL PYLE has taught at Lewis & Clark College and Evergreen State College, both in the Northwest. He is the author of *Wintergreen* (1986), *The Thunder Tree* (1993), and *Where Bigfoot Walks: Crossing the Dark Divide* (1995), all from Houghton Mifflin, as well as many other books about insects and butterflies. Beacon Press will publish a collection of Vladimir Nabokov's butterfly writings co-edited by Mr. Pyle and Brian Boyd.

BRUCE RICE lives in Regina, Saskatchewan. His first collection, *Daniel* (Cormorant Books, 1989) received the Canadian Authors' Association Award for Poetry. A second collection, *Descent Into Lima*, will be published by Coteau Books in the spring of 1996. His poems have been broadcast over Canadian radio and have appeared in several important magazines and anthologies over the past few years. He is a former president of the Saskatchewan Writers' Guild and of the Sage Hill Writing Experience.

DAVID RIVARD's first book of poems, *Torque* (University of Pittsburgh Press, 1987), won the Agnes Lynch Starret Poetry Prize. His second collection, *Hush & Taunt*, will be published by Graywolf Press in the fall of 1996. The winner of many awards and fellowships for his writing, he is a contributing associate at the *Harvard Review* and teaches at Tufts University and in the M.F.A. Writing Program at Vermont College.

SEÁN VIRGO was born in Malta, raised in South Africa and Ireland, and attended boarding school in England. A Canadian citizen since 1972, he has taught literature and creative writing at the Universities of Victoria, Waterloo, York, and Saskatchewan. He is the author of five books of poetry, four volumes of short fiction, and one novel. The winner of numerous awards for his writing in Canada, one of his stories was chosen for *Best American Short Stories* in 1979.

ELLEN BRYANT VOIGT is the author of five books of poetry, including *Claiming Kin* (Wesleyan University Press, 1976), *The Forces of Plenty* (W. W. Norton, 1983), *The Lotus Flowers* (W. W. Norton, 1987), *Two Trees* (W. W. Norton, 1992), and *Kyrie* (W. W. Norton, 1995). The recipient of many awards and prizes for her writing, she currently teaches in the Warren Wilson College low-residency M.F.A. Program for writers and lives in Vermont with her husband and two children.

ACKNOWLEDGMENTS

ALLEN, PAUL: Excerpt from "Letter to Oberg from Pony" by Richard Hugo originally appeared in *31 Letters, 31 Dreams: Poems*, W. W. Norton, © 1977; brief excerpts from Annie Dillard originally appeared in *The Writing Life*, Harper & Row, © 1989; excerpt from "Teaching the 'Nonstandard' Writer" by Richard Kostelanetz originally appeared in *Northwest Review* 28, no. 1, © 1990; excerpt from "To Actualize the Possible: The Writer in the World" by Grace Mojtabai originally appeared in *Nimrod* 27, no. 2, © 1984; short quote from the screenplay, *Cat on a Hot Tin Roof*, by Tennessee Williams was originally published by New Directions, © 1955; Joseph Campbell's term is taken from his *And the Power of Myth*, pt. 4, *Sacrifice and Bliss*, video series, ed. Bill Moyers, Apostrophe S Productions, © 1988; excerpt from "Bitches" by John Ciardi originally appeared in *For Instance*, W. W. Norton, © 1979; "when serpents bargain for the right to squirm" is the title of a poem by e. e. cummings; short passage from the article " 'A Career in the Air Is Like None on the Ground': *Where Shall the Poet Live?*" by Michael Blumenthal originally appeared in *Nimrod* 30, no. 2, © 1987; excerpt from John Donne's "A Valediction Forbidding Mourning" is taken from *The Complete Poetry and Selected Prose of John Donne*, ed. Charles Coffin, The Modern Library, © 1952; Robert Frost's term is taken from *Complete Poems of Robert Frost*, Holt, Rinehart & Winston, © 1949–63; line from "Song of the Open Road" by Walt Whitman is excerpted from *Leaves of Grass*, first published in 1855; excerpt from "Survival" by John Ciardi originally appeared in *Ciardi Himself*, University of Arkansas Press, © 1989; excerpts from Stephen Dunn are taken from his essay "Alert Lovers, Hidden Sides, & Ice Travelers: Notes on Poetic Form & Energy," which originally appeared in *Seneca Review* 20, no. 2, © 1990, and later appeared in Dunn's *Walking Light*, W. W. Norton, © 1994; excerpts from George Oppen originally appeared in "Selections from George Oppen's 'Daybook,'" ed. Dennis Young, *Iowa Review* 18, no. 3, © 1988; excerpt from "The Masterpiece" by Lu Chi, trans. Sam Hamill, originally appeared in full in *Wen Fu: The Art of Writing*, Milkweed Editions, © 1991.

BELL, MARVIN: Jack Gilbert's "In Dispraise of Poetry" is from *Views of Jeopardy*, © 1962 by Jack Gilbert, reprinted with the permission of the author and Alfred A. Knopf, Inc. Excerpt from a poem by Antonio Machado is from the introduction to *Leaping Poetry: An Idea with Poems and Translations by Robert Bly*, Beacon Press, © 1975; Ezra Pound is quoted from his *ABC of Reading*, New Directions, © 1960; Wallace Stevens is quoted from "Of Modern Poetry," a poem originally published in 1942, and subsequently included in Stevens's *Collected Poems*, Vintage Books, © 1990; "The Appren-

by Alice Helen Methfessel, used by permission of the Estate of Elizabeth Bishop and Farrar, Straus & Giroux, Inc., all rights reserved; parts of sentences by Brett Millier are from *Elizabeth Bishop: Life and Memory of It*, University of California Press, © 1993; all quotations of Samuel Taylor Coleridge are from *Biographia Literaria*, first published in 1817.

Thanks are due for the judgment and cooperation of the program directors of the following conferences, all members of Writers' Conferences and Festivals:

Antioch Writers' Workshop
Art of the Wild Conference
Arts and Humanities Council of Tulsa
Asheville Poetry Festival
Aspen Writers' Conference
Bay Area Writers' Workshop
The Bennington Writing Workshops
Blooming Grove Writers' Conference
Bread Loaf Writers' Conference
Cape Cod Writers' Center
Catskill Poetry Workshop
The Charleston Writers' Conference
The Concord Writers' Center
Cuesta College Writers' Conference
Cumberland Valley Fiction Writers' Conference
Environmental Writing Institute
Fine Arts Work Center in Provincetown
Fishtrap, Inc.
Florida Suncoast Writers' Conference
The Frost Place Festival of Poetry
Guadalupe Cultural Arts Center
Haystack Program in the Arts & Sciences / Summer Session
Hofstra University Writers' Conference
Hurston / Wright Foundation Writers' Conference
IMAGINATION Writers' Workshop and Conference
Indiana University Writers' Conference
Iowa Summer Writing Festival
Jackson Hole Writers' Conference
The William Joiner Center Writers' Workshop
Key West Literary Seminar, Inc.

Latin America Writers' Workshop
Legal Workshop for Writers
Napa Valley Writers' Conference
Oklahoma Arts Institute
Open Road Writing Workshops
Oregon's Rock Eagle Writing Festival
Paris Writers' Workshop
Ploughshares International Fiction Writing Seminar
Poets & Writers' Publishing Seminars
Port Townsend Writers' Conference
Prague Writers' Workshop
Rogue Valley Writers' Conference
Santa Fe Writers' Conference
Santa Monica College Writers' Conference
Sewanee Writers' Conference
Snake River Institute
Split Rock Arts Program
Squaw Valley Community of Writers
Stephen Bruno Publishing Inc.
Stonecoast Writers' Conference
Sunken Garden Poets' Conference
Sun Valley Writers' Conference
Taste of Chicago Writing Workshop
Truckee Meadows Community College Writers' Conference
University of North Alabama Writers' Conference
Vermont Studio Center
The Victoria School of Writing
Wesleyan University Writers' Conference
White River Writers' Workshop
Wildacres Writers' Workshop
Writers at Work
The Writers for Racing Project
The Writers and Readers Rendezvous
Yellow Bay Writers' Workshop